The USA in South America
and Other Essays

by Cheddi Jagan

Edited by David Dabydeen
Foreword by Havelock Brewster

First published in 1998 by Hansib Publications Limited
Tower House, 141-149 Fonthill Road, London N4 3HF England

Printed in the United Kingdom by Hillman Printers, Frome

Copyright © Janet Jagan, 1998.
All rights reserved. No part of this publication may be reproduced by any means without the prior written permission of the Publisher.

A CIP record for this book is available from the British Library

ISBN 1-870518-81-0

Dedication

To Ram Karran, and all the thousands of stalwarts who have stood by the People's Progressive Party during the years of long and difficult struggle

ACKNOWLEDGEMENTS

I am grateful once again to Marjorie Davies, Secretary of the University of Warwick's Centre for Caribbean Studies, for her patient and voluntary typing and re-typing of manuscripts; and to Janet Jagan for her exemplary efficiency in supplying materials and answering queries.

Cheddi Jagan was an honoured guest lecturer at the University of Warwick on at least four occasions when he was leader of the Opposition in Guyana. George Lamming wrote of Cheddi Jagan "there is no Caribbean leader who has been so frequently cheated of office; none who has been so grossly misrepresented." At a time when many academics shunned his radical ideas and declined to invite him to their Universities, or to give credence to his People's Progressive Party, I am delighted to acknowledge that Professor Alistair Hennessy (then Director of the Centre for Caribbean Studies) behaved otherwise, giving me, and others, unqualified support in our efforts to provide Dr Jagan with an academic platform in Britain. I owe a profound debt of gratitude to Professor Alistair Hennessy for such generous support.

Professor David Dabydeen
Director, Centre for Caribbean Studies
University of Warwick

Editor's Note

This selection of Cheddi Jagan's essays begins and ends with his revelation of political and electoral corruption in Guyana, and his moving sense of the plight of Guyanese people under the illegal régime of the PNC. The maladministration and kleptomania which Dr Jagan saw as the defining features of the PNC Government were compounded by Cold War politics. The three intervening essays outline Dr Jagan's views of the threat that the American military - industrial complex posed to the stability and security of the Hemisphere, in the Cold War era. When the Cold War ended, Jagan was among the first to seek to establish new and creative relations with the United States of America, and to argue for a new human order which rejected the destructive political conflicts of the past. He was not anti-American in an 'essentialist' manner, but an opponent of policies and practices (many of them underhand) which posed a threat to Third World development, and which denied the revolutionary spirit which gave birth to America ("I cannot but think that the American people who first began that revolution in social and political thought which still moves our world will find sympathy with the ideas and aspirations of my people and Government," he writes to President Kennedy with cool irony - see Appendix).

In preparing these essays for publication I have exercised only a light editorial touch, deleting recurring phrases for instance (Dr Jagan, a copious writer, would sometimes recycle material), or incomplete footnotes. I have not sought to verify or to correct any data in the essays. Given the inadequacy of libraries in Guyana, and the political persecution which limited Dr Jagan's access to information, I find his acquisition and deployment of data remarkable: it is another example of the tenacity of purpose which distinguished his political career, and his ceaseless effort to persuade by reason and by the marshalling of facts (as opposed to the partial truths, propaganda, and verbal bullying which constituted political discourse in Burnhamite Guyana).

Professor David Dabydeen

Contents

Foreword
8

Chapter One
The USA in South America (1968)
13

Chapter Two
Non-Alignment as a Viable Alternative for Regional Co-operation (1982)
35

Chapter Three
The Caribbean is Repelling the Aggressive Course (1984)
81

Chapter Four
Theory of Vital Interests and Security Zones (1984)
99

Chapter Five
Anatomy of Electoral Fraud in Guyana (1986)
147

Appendix
Letter from Premier Cheddi Jagan to President John F Kennedy (1963)
163

Index of Proper Names

174

FOREWORD

"TO SERVE THE REAL INTERESTS OF ALL"

With these words Cheddi Jagan ends the fourth paper in this volume on 'the theory of vital interests and security zones'. They are a good summing-up of his life's struggles, so starkly the antithesis of the 'Western values' he dissects in the paper. The volume contains five papers published between 1968 and 1986. The paper on 'vital interests' is conceptually the centrepiece of the work. The other papers may be viewed as applications in practice of the Western world's theory. Thus Guyana is dealt with (in the first and fifty paper), the Caribbean/Central America (in the third), and the wider international, non-aligned world (in the second).

The papers are very much a product of their time. Much has changed since they were written in ways that would have defied prediction, even of the most visionary. While they are a useful testament to history, they are also, like histories composed not as distant academic exercises but as the immediate *cri de coeur* of those in battle, full of optimism, far beyond any reasonable expectation, strangely insightful of what lies in the future. For example, not withstanding the darkness portrayed of the Reagan cold war era, Jagan found a ray of light opening up for a return to *détente* and peaceful co-existence. And, even more remarkable, saw at that time the convergence of such a potential world development together with the self alienation of PNC supporters, brought about by economic collapse and revolting electoral dishonesty, as providing the basis for change in Guyana. This is then history and prescience born out of whole-hearted dedication to social justice, and sharpened by frustration, anger and deep emotion. To understand better their roots, and contrast with Forbes Burnham, the reader should go to his auto biographical *The West on Trial - My Fight for Guyana's Freedom*.

But not even Jagan's prescience could have anticipated the sea-change that would come upon the world in just a few years. Not merely peaceful co-existence but he collapse of the USSR itself and, as a consequence of that development, the abandonment of pro-Western autocracies, in Guyana and elsewhere, and the democratic return of Jagan's PPP to government - ironically actively aided by ex US President Jimmy Carter of whom at the time Jagan, in some respects, was quite critical.

The centrepiece on the theory of vital interests takes a straightforward Marxist line that the economic interest of the capitalist class determine the West's relationship with the Soviet Union and with emergent socialism all over the world. As illustrated in respect of the 1980's, the deepening tensions "are not due to 'Moscow intrigues' and 'terrorism' but to the general crisis of capitalism which, coupled with the scientific and technological revolution, reproduces its inherent contradiction on an ever growing scale at the centre and periphery". And, the "crisis in the 'Third World' is due not to Soviet expansionism, but to underdevelopment and blatant exploitation and drain of resources under a dependent/distorted capitalist way of 'development'" The West's struggle with communism went through different phases in which a variety of policies were used. From a comprehensive policy of 'containment of communism' under Truman; to Eisenhower's and Dulles's policy of 'peace through strength', and a 'massive retaliation strategy'; to Kennedy's 'limited response' and flexible 'club and carrot' policy; to Jimmy Carter's and Zbigniew Brezezinski's 'differentiated country-to-country approach,' involving isolation of countries not demonstrating independence from Moscow; to Nixon's and Kissinger's policy of *détente*.

By the time Reagan comes onto the scene the United States assesses itself alarmingly as having 'lost positions' all over the non-European world (Afghanistan, Iran, the Middle-East, the Persian Gulf, Central America, the Caribbean, Angola, Ethiopia, Mozambique, and so on). And moreover, as losing out massively to the Soviet Union in the balance of military power. The basis of the latter has been disputed and thought by some to be an exaggeration, if not an invention of the CIA, seized upon for capitalist motives by the weapons producing US multinational corporations. A new and potentially more dangerous cold war era was thus inaugurated. *Détente* was seen as having served only the interest of the Soviet Union. The line taken now was that the Soviet Union was 'an evil empire', that it was a real threat, requiring, if need be, a limited first-strike, nuclear war, that such a war was 'admissible', 'winnable' and survivable.

Guyana, the Caribbean/Central America, and the rest of the (non-aligned) world are situated in the context of this struggle between the West and Soviet Union and the spread of communism. Thus Jagan's interpretation of Guyana's political history since the PPP/PNC split, and particularly since 1968, revolves around the Western and especially the US policy of 'containment of communism', assigning little or no significance to racism in Guyana. He felt strongly about this as I know from several conversations with him in recent years. He felt that he with the PPP was the original and true multiracial leader of Guyana and that Burnham was an unscrupulous, ambitious aberration. As he says in the first essay (1968, "until recently, race was not a serious problem. Indo-Guyanese and Afro-Guyanese for many years had played, worked and lived together amicably." Racial strife, in his view became necessary if Guyana was not to become independent with a PPP Government. In pursuit of capitalist economic interest the US/UK used 'divide and rule' politics which equated with racism and anti-communism.

The extreme to which this approach was carried, the desperation with which it was pursued, is exposed in the fifth paper in which Jagan analyses the anatomy of electoral fraud in Guyana. This paper was published by the *Toronto South Asian Review* and should now be widely read in Guyana as a chastening reminder that such deceit and dishonesty should never again be practised. Jagan goes into a fair amount of statistical detail but the most damning judgement of the 1968 elections comes form Humphrey Taylor, Director of the Opinion Research Centre, London, in a Granada TV film "The Making of a Prime Minister" - "the compilation of the register was a totally dishonest and corrupt operation ....unprecedented for a Commonwealth country ... a pretty awful and disgraceful episode."

The Caribbean/Central America was at that époque of considerable strategic value to the US. It was Reagan who said in 1982 that "the Caribbean Region is a vital strategic and commercial artery for the United States. Nearly half of US trade, two-thirds of our imported oil and over half of our imported strategic minerals pass through the Panama Canal and the Gulf of Mexico. Make no mistake; the well-being and security of our neighbours in this region are in our vital interest." In this essay Jagan basically points to the betrayal of the poor masses of the Caribbean by their political leaders. This is one of Jagan's most scathing pieces. He is undisguisedly contemptuous of the clientism, the pragmatism/opportunism, the puppetry, the corruption, the servility of Caribbean political leaders. He saw them as scrambling for crumbs from the US (e.g. the Caribbean Basin Initiative), engaging in token, petty bourgeois 'localisation', masquerading under labels like 'co-operative socialism', Caribbean integration, the 'middle way', the 'communist threat'. For Vere Bird of Antigua and Barbuda democracy meant little more than getting a US embassy established in the island, a couple of military installations and a Voice of America booster station. Barbados, under Tom Adams, leader of the BLP - reactionary, a defender of colonialism and an opponent of the liberation struggle. The most shameful demonstration of Caribbean puppetry in his view was the invasion of Grenada by the US with the support of most CARICOM states. With all their pious devotion to democracy and justice and freedom Jagan could not overlook the fact that Burnham was most welcome in their midst and they even bank-rolled him to the extent of several hundred million dollars, when they could hardly have been ignorant of the situation in Guyana.

On the international front, the movement that Jagan placed most faith in as offering a viable alternative to domination by the capitalist West was non-alignment. He discusses this in the second paper. Some of the material of this paper overlaps with that of the paper on the theory of vital interest and security zones, but it also presents a useful summary of the history of the Non-Aligned Movement and of its principles. In the present context, the main interest of the paper lies in Jagan's rejection of the concept of 'equidistance' between the two superpowers as the basis of non-alignment. For him, quite clearly there were major differences between the USSR and US which made the former more sympathetic to the development aspirations and struggles for liberation of the underdeveloped countries. Equidistance contradicted history, "linking the oppressor with the oppressed, the exploiter with the exploited." The relevance and strength of non-alignment lay, in his view, in its advocacy of peaceful co-existence, and of course in its support for various Third World causes - anti-colonialism, a new international economic order, and so on.

One could see the importance of the dichotomy to Jagan. Equidistance was not likely to have the effect of rendering obsolete the puppet autocracies supported by the West around the world. But a world of truly peaceful co-existence, even one approximated by a new *détente*, could move things in that direction, as he implied in the final paper on the anatomy of election fraud in Guyana. In the end, neither equidistance nor peaceful coexistence came about, but rather a world dominated by a single capitalist power. The irony was that Jagan was enabled to return to power, after twenty-eight years, democratically elected, but on ideological terms not anticipated in his advocacy of peaceful co-existence.

The significance of this lively and controversial history would be enhanced if we were able to draw from it some useful insights for

Guyana's present situation and future. I will draw two that I think are uppermost in many people's minds - the question of democracy and racism, and economic ideology. Electoral fraud is inexcusable and should never re-occur. It was a shameful episode in our history. But that fraud had its origin, not merely in the ambitions of an opportunistic leader, but in fear of the alternative, real or conjectural, of domination by an Indo-Guyanese majority. Indo-Guyanese have seen the consequences of domination by an Afro-Guyanese minority. They should understand. If that fear is to be legitimised by 'democracy' the results will be no better than the fear that was institutionalised by tyranny.

Race fear is not something peculiar to Guyana. Jagan asserts that before the imperialist contrived split race was not a problem in Guyana. Even if this were so, and there were no external interventions, could such harmony have long survived independence? Almost nowhere in the world do races, or even tribes or religions, live in such numerical democratic contentment - whether it be Malaysia, Fiji, Trinidad and Tobago, Uganda, Kenya, Mauritius, or Rwanda, Congo, Nigeria, or Yugoslavia, Turkey, Ireland, Palestine, Sri Lanka, or the United States. Nature and history do not seem to programme spontaneous racial indifference. We shall have before long to work out constitutional mechanisms that would help to preserve the democratic exercise of political governance.

Democracy has brought with it all over the world a new externally imposed economic tyranny. Jagan did not anticipate such an outcome. He personally never became comfortable with doctrinal capitalism and while bending of necessity to the Northerly winds sought to mould it into an ethic of people-centred development, of poverty reduction, of corporate social responsibility; and also to influence world opinion through his appeal for a New Global Economic Order. Free enterprise too is not programmed to produce spontaneously equitable human development and a fair distribution of income and wealth. We shall have before long to set in place those mechanisms that implement our commitment to economic democracy. Are these not rainbows worth chasing after?

Havelock Brewster
Brussels
15 December 1997

Chapter One

The USA in South America

The late Aneurin Bevan in his book, *In Place of Fear*, wrote that fear of communism caused Americans to have a distorted view of the world and the forces at play in modern-day society.

This observation is borne out by a Congressional Report by Congressman Armistead Selden and William S Malliard, two members of the House of Representatives Foreign Affairs Committee, who visited Guyana last November as part of a Latin American study mission.

The Congressmen remarked that "Guyana's ability to pursue development schemes and attract international private and public capital will depend in large measure upon resolution of the racial issue which plagues the country," and that Guyana's political problems stemmed from "the manoeuvres of professed Marxist Cheddi Jagan and his wife."

From this report, one would come to the conclusion that we were the formenters of racism and were the stumbling blocks to development and progress.

Actually, the root cause of our present racial and other problems is Anglo-American Cold War conspiracy to destroy the People's Progressive Party (PPP). Today, US-dictated fiscal, trade and economic policies are the main reasons for stagnation, dissatisfaction and unrest.

US intervention in our domestic affairs was brought out into the open in the 1967 exposé of the CIA. The London *Sunday Times,* on April 16, in a story headlined 'How the CIA Got Rid of

Jagan', said: "As coups go, it was not expensive; over five years the CIA paid out something over £25,000. For the colony, British Guiana, the result was about 170 dead, untold hundreds wounded, roughly £10 million-worth of damage to the economy and a legacy of racial bitterness."

On Sunday, April 23, a reader, Leslie C Stone, wrote the *Sunday Times* stating that we were responsible for the racialism and bloodshed. In reply, the *Insight* team said: "The racial strife was fairly amicable, except for relatively minor scuffles between hotheads in 1962, until the 1963 strike divided the country. Nor would the 1964 battles in the sugarfields have been so protracted and bloody, but for the legacy of racial bitterness."

On the same date, the *Sunday Times Insight* Team carried another exposé headlined 'Macmillan, Sandys backed CIA anti-Jagan plot'. Implicated were Harold Macmillan, former Prime Minister; Duncan Sandys, former Commonwealth and Colonial Secretary; two top security men in Britain and a number of British officials in Guyana. It said that "not all the British officials on the spot were happy with what the Americans were doing" ... with "such massive manipulation of the local political scene. This feeling was strengthened by the fact that the CIA's efforts were worsening the colony's already severe racial difficulties; the Africans supported Burnham and the Indians supported Jagan, and tension between the two racial groups grew as the CIA levered the two sides further apart. (Eventually, this broke out in bloodshed)".

The story also asserted that "the CIA were also operating under consular cover in Guyana".

This should explain:

> 1) The refusal by the Governor to carry out the request of the PPP Council of Ministers for the expulsion in 1963 of Howard MacCabe, CIA agent, and the delay in expelling in 1962, Dr Joost Sluis of the Christian Anti-Communist Crusade.

2) The failure of the Commissioner of Police to take effective action against demonstrators, trade union and political leaders who violated the Proclamation Order prohibiting demonstrations in the restricted area surrounding the Parliament Building, and against those who were associated with a secret illegal radio transmitter found in a van owned by d'Aguiar Bros. Ltd, a company owned and controlled by Peter d'Aguiar (leader of the reactionary United Force and until September, 1967, Minister of Finance) and his family.

3) The delay by the Governor, Sir Ralph Grey, in bringing out at crucial times during 1962 and 1963, the British armed forces to aid the police in maintaining law and order.

4) The failure to break up the PNC (the party of the now Prime Minister, L F S Burnham) terrorist organization, although the Governor and the Commissioner of Police knew of its insurrectionary plan X13. This terrorist gang was later responsible for the loss of many lives and for the destruction of government property by dynamite.

5) The failure of the Commissioner of Police to bring to the notice of myself (as Premier) and the PPP Minister of Home Affairs two documents, compiled in August and September of 1963 by the Security Branch, entitled '*Research Paper on the PNC Terrorist Organization,*' which named fifty people including top-ranking PNC leaders and activists and an American agent J O'Keefe, of whom twenty-five were recommended for prosecution but were never charged.

6) The order made through emergency regulations by the Governor, Sir Richard Luyt, suppressing the '*Research paper on the PNC Terrorist Organisation,*' and making its

possession a criminal offence subject to a fine of £500 and/or six months imprisonment.

7) The continuous police harassment and searching of PPP leaders and activists, including the Minister of Natural Resources, and the detention of PPP legislators by the Governor to prevent Parliament from functioning - all aimed at creating the impression abroad that the PPP was responsible for the disturbances and riots.

8) The Governor's intervention in the 1964 election, and the changing of electoral procedure permitting extensive use of proxy voting, which was highly criticized by the Commonwealth Team of Observers.

RACE, CLASS AND LIBERATION

Colonialists and imperialists never had any scruples about creating divisions and even committing murder if these means were necessary for the maintenance of their political rule and economic domination. The British in their long history of Empire were adept at divide-and-rule - one religion against another, one tribe against another, one race against another.

In Guyana, racism and anti-communism have been the main weapons used by Anglo-American imperialism to 'contain' and destroy the Guyana liberation movement.

In 1953, our Constitution was suspended and the PPP Government was forcibly expelled from office on the excuse that it was setting up a one-party, Communist state. Nearly a decade later, at the October 1963 Independence Conference, Duncan Sandys refused to fix a date for independence and changed our electoral system. He charged that "racialism was the curse to British Guiana today" and attributed blame for the turmoil to the development of party politics along racial lines. "In the present acute form, this (racialism) can be traced to the split in the country's main political party in 1955. It was then that the People's Progressive Party, which had previously drawn its support from both the main races, broke into two bitterly opposed political groups, the one predominantly Indian led by Dr Jagan, and the other predominantly African, led by Mr Burnham."

What Sandys failed to mention was that the split of the PPP in 1955 was engineered by the Churchill-led British government. This is what succeeded in destroying the unity of the major ethnic groups and the united front against colonialism. Even the Robertson Commission, appointed to whitewash the suspension of the Constitution, admitted this unity. In its reports in 1954, it said:

> It was largely by the efforts of Dr and Mrs Jagan that the PPP was built up and *kept united...* In this way racial dissension between African and East Indian elements was minimized and by the time of the election campaign in 1953 a useful political instrument was forged.

Until recently, 'race' was not a serious problem. Indo-Guyanese and Afro-Guyanese for many years had played, worked and lived together amicably. The Commonwealth Commission which looked into the CIA-fomented disturbances of 1962 remarked:

> We found little evidence of any racial segregation in the social life of the country, and in Georgetown. East Indians and Africans seemed to mix and associate with one another on terms of the greatest cordiality, though it was clear that the recent disturbances and the racial twist given to them by some of the unprincipled and self-seeking politicians had introduced slight, but it is hoped, transient overtones of doubt and reserve.

> But we are merely drawing attention to the circumstances mentioned above in order to show that there is no clear-cut division between the races and that although, broadly

speaking, Dr Jagan's supporters are for the most part East Indians and the supporters of PNC are drawn mostly from the African races, the difference is not really racial, but economic and vocational.

But economic and vocational differences were there to be exploited by unscrupulous politicians. The Robertson Commission talked about "the fears of the African section of the population." And Burnham, to work on these fears, joined up, after his defeat at the 1957 general election, with the conservative and reactionary United Democratic Party (UDP) led by John Carter (now Guyana's Ambassador to Washington) and Rudy Kendall (now Minister of Health), who headed the racist League of Coloured People. (Carter, Kendall, Lionel Luckhoo, now Guyana's High Commissioner to London, and businessmen John Fernandes and John Dare, prior to 1957 were dubbed traitors by Burnham for leading a delegation to London in October 1953 to praise the British government for suspending our Constitution and removing us from the government).

Burnham's alliances with conservative and racist elements resulted in the class struggle appearing not, as previously in the 1920's, as Coloured (Indians, Negroes, Mixed) against White, but as Indian against Negro and Mixed. Fears of one kind or another, whether real or imagined, were generated against the PPP and expressed in racial and anti-communist terms.

The People's Progressive Party and the PPP governments were dubbed as Indian. Our 1960-64 development programme, which was heavily weighted towards agriculture and drainage and irrigation, was deemed to be essentially designed to help Indians.

But the Commonwealth Commission of 1962 saw through this and commented:

> The political professions of the PNC were somewhat vague and amorphous. There was a tendency to give a racial tinge to its policy. Mr Burnham expressed the opinion that it was Dr Jagan who was responsible for this unfortunate development.

We do not, however, think that there is much substance in the contention of Mr Burnham and it seems to us that whatever racial differences existed were brought about by political propaganda.

US INTERVENTION

Political propaganda and racial strife became necessary if Guyana was not to become independent with a PPP government. (The 1960 London Constitutional Conference had clearly stated that independence would follow the 1961 general election, which we had won despite some gerrymandering by a British government-appointed Electoral Boundary Commissioner.) This was largely achieved by US intervention under the Kennedy Administration. Obsessed by developments in Cuba, Washington conspired with Burnham to bring down the PPP government.

Arthur Schlesinger, Jr. admits in his book, *A Thousand Days*, that after a conversation with Burnham in Washington in May 1962, he recommended to the late President Kennedy that the United States should back Burnham, and that the way to destroy the PPP Government was by the introduction of proportional representation. And Drew Pearson, the American columnist, reported on March 22, 1964, that Kennedy made a special trip to London in the summer of 1963 to see Harold Macmillan to persuade him not to grant independence to Guyana. According to Drew Pearson, the 1963 strike was secretly inspired by a combination of United States CIA money and British Intelligence and gave London the excuse it wanted for withholding independence and changing our electoral system.

In the 1964 election, the CIA intervened with money. According to the *New York Times* of April 28, 1966, the CIA "has poured money into Latin American election campaigns in support of moderate candidates and against leftist leaders such as Cheddi Jagan of British Guiana."

The *Sunday Times* story of April 23, 1967, stated that the CIA resorted to corrupt means to split my party. It took out an insurance policy for "one ex-Jagan supporter for $30,000 in 1964." This is in line with bribes to a number of trade unionists who received money from the American Institute for Free Labour Development, another CIA - backed organization, that is today in charge of the Critchlow Labour Institute which provides trade union education in Guyana.

It is little wonder that Guyana is today a land of bribery, corruption, nepotism, 'squandermania' and racial discrimination. The main motivation is selfishness and get-rich-quick. Anyone willing to maintain the old order, no matter how corrupt he or she may be, can climb to the top.

The Deputy Lord Mayor of the capital, Georgetown, a government supporter, in a broadcast in May 1967 cried out against a new elite creating "a new, larger area of snobbery," and bribery which "is all over the place and is fast becoming a national industry ... the harm done in any situation in which bribery, corruption, nepotism and favouritism assume national proportions and is a way of life from top down, can never be calculated."

The Civil Service Association, which helped to bring the coalition parties in the government, in August, 1967, accused the government of causing a breach of industrial principle and a display of gross irresponsibility and arrogance. It appealed to the Trade Union Council to "intercede before it's too late."

As regards the economic situation, Guyana is in a state of stagnation and near bankruptcy. The Government cannot meet its day-to-day financial obligations. The Government openly admitted that it owed the commercial banks £15 million, which should have been paid by December 31, 1966, and £2 million in Treasury Bills.

Meanwhile, concessions are made to the rich. Our timber, bauxite and oil resources have been turned over to foreign monopolies. Capital taxes introduced by the PPP Government in 1962 were abolished or drastically modified in 1965, and higher consumer taxes were imposed in 1966 and 1967.

There has been a general decline in the standard of living.

The cost-of-living index figure has jumped by eight points in 1965 and 1966. This leap is in sharp contrast to the 10-point increase in the previous eight year period, 1956-1964. This year the increase will be staggering when the full impact is realized of the 1967 taxes, which aimed at raising twice as much money as the 1966 taxes. Increased rents have also added to the misery caused by rising prices, growing unemployment and underemployment.

While the cost of living continues to rise, wages and salaries for the middle and lower categories have either remained stagnant or have risen only moderately. Sawmill, forest and quarry workers, for instance, received during the PPP regimé the same minimum wage as government unskilled workers. Now the government has fixed only £3.50 and £3.52 per day as compared with £4.00 for government workers.

The government's trading policies have also contributed to the worsened position of the people. Pressed by the US Government, the coalition has placed restrictions on cheaper imported goods from the socialist countries. This has contributed to higher prices. By abandoning trade with Cuba, Guyana has lost a valuable and profitable market for our export of rice and timber. This in turn has affected the position of rice farmers, loggers, forest and sawmill workers.

Faced with budgetary problems, the government has also slashed social services - education, health, pensions - and reduced spending for crop purchases, crop bonuses and other forms of help to farmers. Farmers have suffered a drop in income as a result of the fall in prices of their crops - rice, plantains, milk, coffee and citrus. The fall in income has meant less money in the hands of farmers and workers, and this has affected business turnover, estimated in 1966 to be 30 per cent less than the average for 1964 and 1965.

That the economy is stagnant has been well summed up in the words of a strong government supporter, businessman John Fernandes, when he recently lamented: "economically we are in a bad way and no one seems to care."

GUYANA IS NO MODEL

But Guyana propagandists are busy at home and abroad painting a rosy picture. Recently, the London *Daily Telegraph* praised the coalition government for achieving an 8 per cent rate of increase in the gross domestic product for 1966, and he recommended that its economic planning should be a model for Africa.

Actually the 8 per cent growth rate is largely fictitious. *The Bank of Guyana Report* for 1966 reduced this to a net figure of 3 per cent after making a deduction of 5 per cent, 2 per cent for price increases and 3 per cent for population increase. For 1967, the net figure would be zero as the *Economic Survey of Guyana* (1966) predicts that the growth rate "would probably be in the region of 4 per cent or 5 per cent over 1966."

The high growth rate for 1966 was largely due to increased activity in mining (bauxite) and government outlay on infrastructure - construction of roads, sea defences, airports, public buildings, harbours and stellings. The productive sectors - manufacturing and agriculture - performed poorly. The share of agriculture, including livestock, declined from 22.2 per cent of GDP in 1962, 24 per cent in 1963, 21.4 per cent in 1964 (the worst year of disturbances), 20.5 per cent in 1965, to only 19 per cent in 1966.

Manufacturing showed slight increase, "although the rate of expansion was slowing down." Consequently, the *Bank of Guyana Report*, putting it mildly, stated: "Guyana's economic growth rate was thus not as broadly based as might have been desirable."

As regards the future, bauxite production cannot continue to expand at the same rate as over the last two years.[1] Nor can government expenditure on infrastructure be maintained at the present level without grave consequences such as increase in imports, particularly of foods (£28.7 million in 1964, £30.7 million in 1965 and £33.4 million in 1966), rise in prices, increased cost of living, growing debt charges, and budgetary and balance-of-payments deficits.

Balance-of-payments on current accounts have changed from a surplus of £26.4 million in 1963 to a deficit of £27.9 million in

1966, and a "larger current account deficit is forecast for 1967."

The 1967 budget was brought into balance by consumer taxes on the poor and financial juggling - diverting grants and loans from the British government for the capital budget to the current budget.

Debt charges have jumped from 12 per cent of the budget in 1960 to 16 per cent in 1966. With another 44 per cent being squandered in salaries for the government's over-bloated bureaucracy, only an inadequate 40 per cent remains for health, education, pensions, subsidies, crop bonuses and guaranteed minimum prices to farmers.

But the 40 per cent is likely to drop to 26 per cent in the early 1970's when debt charges will be about 30 per cent of the budget. Then, in order to maintain social services at existing levels, more taxes will fall on the poor, and Guyana, like Latin American countries, will be forced to borrow not for development, but to pay debts falling due. In 1956, Latin American countries borrowed $540 million (US) and handed back an exact amount as debt payments.

The Guyana model of economic planning and development is based on *Operation Bootstrap* of Puerto Rico, which has certain distinct advantages over other so-called Third World countries - US runaway capitalists have the advantage of low wages in Puerto Rico; goods produced in Puerto Rico enter duty-free into the United States; Puerto Ricans can migrate without restrictions into the USA; millions of dollars collected from duties on rum are returned to Puerto Rico.

Yet Puerto Rico is still plagued with poverty and unemployment and all the ills of a colonial society. Despite the ballyhoo and the US attempt to make Puerto Rico into a showpiece, the national income per head of population is lower than that of the poorest US state.

Other Third World territories which have followed the Puerto Rican model at US dictation are also in deep trouble. Jamaica, like Guyana, boasts of a wonderful performance of its economy - an increase in the gross domestic product between 1950 and 1965 at an annual rate of 7.2 per cent. But for the three successive five-year periods, there was a progressive decline in per capita national income - 7 per cent for 1950-55; 3.7 per cent for 1955-60; and 3 per cent for 1960-65.

Jamaica, in common with other British Commonwealth countries, is plagued with growing tensions and problems, chief among which are unemployment, inequality of income and balance-of-payments deficits.

Commenting on the grave unemployment situation in Trinidad, the *Trinidad Guardian* on August 9, 1967, wrote:

> One hundred jobs in Canada. The possibility of three hundred in Puerto Rico. A steady trickle of domestics to North America. A fairly large flow of skilled and professional peoples to Canada. These are the avenues being used or explored in a society where the rate of unemployment may not be the worst in the world, but is nonetheless unbearable.

Clearly, the Guyana model of economic planning and development is not model for Africa or for any other Third World area or country. There will be no real progress as long as Guyana is tied to fiscal, trade and economic policies dictated by Washington and big business at home and abroad. Indeed, conditions will inevitably worsen with growing disillusionment, dissatisfaction and frustration. 'Lucian,' a strong government supporter, writing in the *Sunday Graphic* of July 16, 1967, said:

> Many people - Guyanese and non-Guyanese - are disgusted with the present state of affairs in this country. Some are packing up to leave out of sheer frustration, while others are dejected from unbearable disgust.

IDEOLOGICAL STRUGGLE

As conditions deteriorate, Guyanese and West Indians are being told by the apologists and ideologues for imperialism and neo-colonialism that the cause of their suffering lies in themselves;

that they are inefficient and unproductive; that they have not acquired enough skills; that capital is short, and in the words of Prime Minister, L F S Burnham, that they must "eat less, sleep less and work harder"; that they must curb their excessive birth rate; that they must come together in larger groupings because their population is too small to provided an adequate internal market.

The objectives of the imperialists are threefold: to cast blame on the working class for the failures of the ruling capitalist class; to dangle fresh 'carrots'; to extend US hegemony - political, economic and military - over territories where Britain and other European competitors once held sway.

The vehicle by which these objectives are to be attained is the Organization of American States (OAS) and Caribbean unity - a Caribbean Free Trade Area (CARIFTA) or a Common Market. Entry into the OAS is touted as a means of cashing in on aid from the Alliance for Progress and on loans from the Inter-American Development Bank. Caribbean unity is held out as the only hope for viability and progress.

Unity and integration are essential if the purpose is to break with imperialism and neo-colonialism. But this is not the kind of unity contemplated. What is projected is the strengthening of the position of foreign capital, particularly US capital.

And the big drive for common markets and free trade areas in different parts of the world is motivated mainly by the desire of US big business to surmount tariff walls of nation-states. Note the candid observation of Mr George Ball, former Under-secretary of State, now Chairman of the big investment banking firm, Lehman Bros. International Ltd. Addressing the New York Chamber of Commerce recently, he said:

> The multi-national US corporation is ahead of, and in conflict with, existing world political organizations represented by the nation state. Major obstacles to the multi-national corporation are evident in Western Europe, Canada and a good part of the developing world.

Observe this comment about the European Common Market from a newsletter circulated by the private West German banks, Merck, Fink & Co. And Waldthausen:

> When Britain becomes a member of the EEC, several thousand US companies which are already established with their own British subsidiaries in the UK will also enjoy the benefits of this continental market.
>
> They will be able to mesh and synchronize their investments and operations in Britain and on the continent so as to quickly develop an all-European plan for their production and sales. In view of the size of their direct investment ... generally speaking the Americans are in a better position than their British or European competitors immediately to exploit the advantages of an expanded Common Market.

US multi-national corporations will like not only to take over Europe, but also to cement the chains of neo-colonialism in the Caribbean and at the same time to displace their British, French and Dutch competitors.

That no fundamental change is intended in the Caribbean was clearly pointed out by the Incorporated Commonwealth Chambers of Industry and Commerce after their delegation met the Prime Minister and other Trinidad experts and advisers. Throwing in the red-herring of communism, the delegation wrote:

> Communist infiltration: it was felt that the danger of communist infiltration in the area should not be regarded lightly and the earlier situation in Guyana was referred to. The delegation was asked to bear the problem in mind and to emphasize in their talks the importance of preserving the traditional system of free enterprise.

Neither the kind of Caribbean unity contemplated nor the OAS will cure the ills of Caribbean society or bring salvation to the people of this region. Latin American countries which are members of the OAS and served by the Alliance for Progress and the Inter-American Bank are in continuous trouble.

As long ago as 1961, at the Punta del Este Conference, when the Alliance for Progress was inaugurated, the objective was to eradicate poverty, illiteracy and backwardness. An economic growth rate of 2.6 per cent was projected, at a time when the average figure for Western Europe was 3.5 per cent and for the socialist bloc 7 - 9 per cent. But even the limited expectations have not materialized. In fact, there has been a steady decline. The average figure for 1960 to 1965 was 1.6 per cent as compared with 1.7 per cent for the period 1955-1960 and 2.2 per cent for the period 1950 to 1955. Argentina, one of the most developed countries in Latin America, suffered a decline of 2.7 per cent in the gross product for 1966.

Little wonder that Dom Helder Camara, Archbishop of Rio de Janeiro, said some time ago that the Alliance was dead.

Even in the fields of housing, health and education in which the Alliance was supposed to concentrate, there has been failure. In 1961, the housing deficiency in Argentina was estimated to be 15 million houses. According to the Inter-American Bank of Development, the need in 1966 was 19 million houses, 4 million more than at the start of the plan.

There are also balance of payments problems, runaway inflation and devaluation of currency. In 1961, the official rate was 250 pesos; in the black market, it was 290 pesos. In Brazil and Chile, inflationary rise was greater than in Argentina. The currency of Uruguay lost 90 per cent of its value during 1965 and 1966.

US aid alone is not the answer. South American countries received $500 million in 1962 under the Alliance, but lost exactly the same amount in that year because of falling prices.

More capital flows out of, than comes into, South America. According to figures of the Economic Commission for Latin America (ECLA), for every dollar invested by North Americans in the period 1946 to 1956, there was an outflow of 3.17 dollars.

In Guyana, profits of more than £50 million are made annually by foreign investors. For Jamaica, net outgoing profits for 1964 were $52 million (WI) while new investments were a mere $22 million; for 1965, the outflow increased to about $50 million.

And we know from our own experience that about 80 cents out of every dollar of US aid is tied to purchases of goods and services from the USA.

This kind of conditional aid also has other strings. Recipient countries are forced to tailor their monetary, fiscal and exchange policies to suit the US Treasury and the International Monetary Fund (IMF).

For instance, under an agreement signed in November 1965, the US Treasury and the IMF have what amounted to virtual control of Colombia's policies. When the new President, Carlos Lleras Restrepo, was asked to renew the agreement, to repel the recently imposed exchange restrictions and to devalue the peso, he refused, charging that the IMF's demands "overstepped the limits of national sovereignty."

Countries receiving US aid are also forced on development of infrastructure and social overheads. This in time leads to crushing debt burdens.

The answer to the economic ills facing Guyana, the Commonwealth Caribbean territories, Latin America and other Third World countries, is not to chase after rainbows.

The OAS must be recognized for what it is - a cold-war military alliance, founded in 1948 and based upon the economic foreign policy objectives of the Truman Doctrine of 1947.

This doctrine aimed not only at the destruction of socialism but also at the maintenance of the economic status quo of colonialism and neo-colonialism. It opposed planned economics and government control of foreign trade, and equated democracy and freedom with the free enterprise capitalist system, the "American way of life," which could "survive in America only if it became a world system."

Under this doctrine, the Latin American economy has been placed in a strait-jacket as a raw material producer with an economy in imbalance, dependent on the export of one crop or one mineral.

What is needed in Guyana, Latin America and other Third World countries is the end of foreign political, military and economic domination and the restructuring of the economy in the interest of the people.

Revolutionary changes necessary

Third World countries would do well to compare the social and economic progress of Cuba with other Latin American countries, and of China with India and other Southeast Asian countries.

As against the progressive decline in Latin America, Cuba is moving ahead. As long ago as December 31, 1963, the *New York Times* commented:

> The Castro regimé is certainly strong and possibly stronger than ever... There is no apparent weakening of Premier Castro's appeal inside Cuba or of his stature as a world figure... All children are getting some education; the great bulk are being well-fed and taken care of, however poor their parents. The Negro and mulatto population is getting genuine equality. The Government leaders are untainted by any fiscal scandals... To have survived five years was a remarkable feat whose explanation is far more complicated than attributing it solely to Soviet-bloc help.

Those who propound the view that inefficiency, low level of technical skill, shortage of capital, 'population explosion,' and the small size of population and territory are the main factors responsible for backwardness and poverty have evidently not examined China and India. India became politically free in 1947, the Chinese Communist party assumed power in 1949. Both started out with about the same level of technical skill. The 'population explosion' in both countries is about the same. In terms of geography and size of population, both are huge.

Yet India which received more foreign aid than China is today on the verge of starvation and bankruptcy; hundreds of thousands of people will die from hunger. The devaluation of the Indian rupee by 33 1/3 per cent has not helped the situation. It has been reported that India has reached the point where it would soon be unable to meet its debt payments, a position long ago met by Latin American countries.

The Bank of Baroda in its *Weekly Review* of August 21, 1967, wrote:

> The Indian economy has now been passing through a very critical period. While the agricultural sector is in a perilous state thanks to two successive droughts, the industrial economy is afflicted with recession on a scale unknown hitherto.
>
> The declaration of the growth of industrial production in the last two years may be termed as stagnation. Recession, on the other hand, is a recent phenomenon which represents a climate of chronic stagnation in the past few years and has proved to be more far-reaching in terms of its undesirable economic consequences.

China, on the other hand, despite its internal political turmoil, has been making rapid strides. Little wonder that the *Washington Post*, editorializing on July 3, 1967, on the Congressional Joint Economic Committee's Special study of the Chinese economy, stated:

> Far from being the land of total chaos and conflict, China is ... a country which has made considerable progress in the past and which continues to tackle major economic concerns.

The Committee's study is the most comprehensive and timely one available. Its central conclusions summarized in Chairman Proximire's report, are that China is in a "reasonably satisfactory food situation with no indication of food stringency," that "remarkable gains" in education is limited not by its economic resources but its technical know-how (itself "not inconsiderable and expanding"). "China's recent explosion of a thermonuclear bomb underscores this assessment of its nuclear progress."

The reason for China's advance is rooted in the basic fact that the Chinese in 1949 expelled the foreign exploiters, nationalized the mines, factories, plantations, banks, insurance companies and trade firms owned by the imperialists and their Chinese collaborators, the "comprador" capitalists, and took away the land from the warlords and landlords and gave it to the exploited landless peasants.

India, on the other hand, suffered a decline because from the time of independence up to this day, it was saddled not only with the big foreign exploiters, but also with big local capitalists, zamindars and taluhdars, Besides, it carried on its back a huge burden of defence, a legacy of the Cold War and Partition.

Clearly social and economic progress for Guyana, the Caribbean, Latin America and other Third World countries depends on a scientific approach to economic planning and the adoption of a revolutionary policy and programme which should include:

> 1) Nationalization of the commanding heights of the economy - all foreign owned factories, mines, plantations, banks and insurance, electricity, telephone and telegraph companies;
>
> 2) Drastic land reform;
>
> 3) Rigid system of exchange and price controls;
>
> 4) Simultaneous expansion of industry and agriculture in the public and co-operative sectors; and
>
> 5) Genuine democracy and involvement of the masses at all levels.

Naturally, such a programme, already embarked upon by some Third World countries in Africa and Asia, has been and will be opposed by the imperialists and neo-colonialists, who are wedded to the free enterprise system, to the Truman Doctrine of "containment," and to the Johnson Doctrine of "liberation" and "massive intervention."

Whenever the free enterprise, capitalist system is threatened, the US government will use the chosen instrument of its foreign policy, the CIA, for covert subversion and violence. And when it becomes necessary, marines will overtly land as in the Dominican Republic and Vietnam.

To the American ruling class and the industrial - military complex, political science has been reduced from ballots to bullets, to simple gangsterism.

It is incumbent on all revolutionary movements to develop a disciplined, ideologically-sound party, to wage a many-sided struggle and to be prepared to meet imperialist force with revolutionary force.

In Guyana, the working class is fighting in defence of its vital interests. In 1965, there was a record-breaking 146 industrial strikes. In 1966, the total was 172 and up to the end of April 1967, the number was already 57.

The Government's answer to the wave of industrial strikes and seething discontent is threats and intimidation. It has already passed a National Security Act, under which anyone can be restricted or detained indefinitely without trial. Now it is proposing to enact anti-strike legislation in the form of what is to be compulsory, but now voluntary, arbitration.

It is subverting the Constitution by undermining and bypassing such independent Constitutional bodies as the Public Service Commission, Police Service Commission and the Elections Commission. By forcing the resignation of the former Chief Justice, by summarily dismissing the most top-ranking Guyanese Officer of the Defence Force, and by prematurely retiring the Guyanese Commissioner of Police the Government is inexorably moving towards the establishment of a police state.

Steps are now being taken to rig the next general elections which are due to be held in late 1968. The registration machinery is now being taken out of the hands of the Elections Commission and put completely under the control of the Minister of Home Affairs (police and security) who is being aided by a US company, Shoup International. Apart from the padding of the local electoral roll, extensive fraud will be perpetrated by the unprecedented decision to permit all Guyanese abroad, no matter how long absent, to become voters. US Congressmen and policy makers may glibly talk about freedom, democracy and progress. But the evidence is abundant that Washington is leading this country to a dictatorship. When the struggle for national liberation sharpens here, as it inevitably will, true and genuine American Democrats must know who is to be blamed and which side to be on.

(*Freedomways*, First Quarter, 1968, pp. 24 - 40)

[1] Actually, in early October, the Demerara Bauxite Company, a subsidiary of the Aluminium Company of Canada, informed the Guyana Mine Workers Union that in the "forseeable future", there would be a 20% cut-back in the production of metal grade bauxite. The Union President claimed that the cut-back would mean a reduction of some 10% of the company's overall production.

CHAPTER TWO

NON-ALIGNMENT AS A VIABLE ALTERNATIVE FOR REGIONAL CO-OPERATION[1]

The Non-Aligned Movement (NAM) has proved to be a constructive force in the cause of liberation, peace and social progress. During the past 20 years, it has helped to focus attention on the most burning issues and to contribute significantly to the extension of peoples' struggle for decolonisation and the elimination of the vestiges of colonialism, neo-colonialism, apartheid and racial discrimination; for a new and just political and economic order; for the transfer of technology; for the strengthening of the role of the United Nations; for the establishment of international economic norms of inter-state relations on the basis of peaceful co-existence and respect for national sovereignty, equality and mutual respect; for disarmament and the security of nations.

Can the Non-Aligned Movement now be a viable alternative for regional co-operation in a very aggravated world situation, particularly in the Caribbean and Central America, and in the context of the U S re-invocation of the Monroe Doctrine and the Roosevelt corollary 'big stick' and cold war methods? The answer to this question depends on the extent to which firstly the NAM's unity cohesiveness and solidarity are maintained and its principles and goals are adhered to; secondly, the political will displayed by NAM leaders to stand up to the threats and pressures of imperialism at this time of grave economic and social crisis caused by the recession in the capitalist world, burdensome debt, and budget and balance of payments deficits in non-aligned countries; and thirdly, the NAM seeing the necessity to work with other progressive, peace and revolutionary movements for the achievement of unity of the three world revolutionary streams - the socialist community, the national liberation movement and the working class and democratic forces in the developed capitalist countries.

Antecedents of the NAM

The Non-Aligned Movement emerged under special circumstances. It has its roots in World War II, the Asian People's Conference in New Delhi in 1947, the Conference of the Colombo Powers in 1954 and the Conference of 29 Asian and African states in Bandung, Indonesia in 1955.

The Second World War, fought for the preservation of freedom and democracy, gave a big impetus to the anti-colonialist and anti-imperialist revolution. It ended with the defeat of fascism, the liberation of the Eastern European states, the independence of India (dismembered by the creation of Pakistan), Burma and Ceylon (now Sri Lanka), and a decisive shift in the world balance of forces against imperialism. From one socialist state after the 1917 Great October Socialist Revolution, there emerged a world socialist system and the struggle for national and social liberation sharpened.

A counter-offensive was launched against the powerful wave for liberation and emancipation of peoples in order to restore the old mode of international relations based on privilege, oppression and exploitation. In the Far East, the colonialist powers returned to resume control: the French in Indochina, the Dutch in Indonesia, and the British in Malaya (now Malaysia) in a barbaric war involving Gurkah troops and Dyak hunters, with prices on the heads of communist patriots who had helped to expel the Japanese fascist invaders.

Emerging from the war as the most powerful capitalist state, the USA abandoned the 'Good Neighbour' policy of President Franklin D Roosevelt. The close relationship and co-operation which had been developed in the fight against fascism was changed after the death of Roosevelt in 1944 into an anti-communist crusade and cold war. The USA embarked on a course, to prevent by whatever means at its disposal, national and social revolutions, and became the international policeman in defence of the old order and the maintenance of the status quo.

At Baylor University on March 6, 1947, President Harry Truman made a speech on foreign economic policy which clearly stated that governments which conducted planned economies and controlled foreign trade were dangers to freedom; that freedom of speech and worship were dependent on the free enterprise system. He declared that controlled economies were "not the American way" and "not the way of peace". He urged that "the whole world should adopt the American system" and that "the American system could survive in America only if it became a World System". Calling for action, he implored: "Unless we act and act decisively, it [government-controlled economy and government-controlled foreign trade] will be the pattern of the next century ... if this trend is not reversed, the Government of the United States will be under pressure, sooner or later, to use these same devices to fight for markets and for raw materials."[2]

Wartime co-operation was abruptly brought to a halt. During World War II, the Soviet Union, USA, Britain and France together fought successfully against Germany, Italy and Japan. In the fight for freedom and democracy, the equation was liberal capitalism and communism against fascism (decadent and terroristic state-monopoly capitalism). In the subsequent cold war period, the equation changed. Fascism was no longer the enemy for the West; it became an ally. Communism became the common enemy; it was regarded as a 'disease' which had to be 'contained', and if possible eradicated. John Foster Dulles[3] equated fascism and communism, and some in a more refined definition condemned "dictatorships of the right and the left."

The instruments created were the Central Intelligence Agency (CIA) in 1948 for overt and covert action, and under treaties with US client states, a world-wide 'iron ring' of military bases for the encirclement of the Soviet Union and other socialist states - the Rio Pact in 1947; the North Atlantic Treaty Organisation (NATO) in April 1949; The Baghdad Pact on February 24, 1955 (later the Central Treaty Organisation after the revolution of 1958 led to Iraq's withdrawal); the South East Asia Treaty Organisation (SEATO) on September 8, 1954, after the communist victory in China in 1949, the US fiasco in Korea in 1950-51, and the disastrous French defeat at Dien Bien Phu in Vietnam in 1954. The 'big stick' once again became a decisive factor in US foreign policy.

Under successive administrations, the cold-war policy of 'containment of communism' took on new interpretations - preventive war, liberation, brinkmanship and massive retaliation. The resultant effects were manifold - the sabotage and the emasculation of the United Nations; aid with strings; a gigantic arms race and the arming of West Germany; McCarthyism and red witch-hunting in the United States and elsewhere; the support of reactionary regimes; and the use of force and fraud against genuine national liberation movements.

On the fiction that the Soviet Union was preparing to launch a war and that Latin America was threatened by communist aggression from within and without, President Truman, in the ensuing hysteria, called in May 1946 for the military unification of the continent.

At the February 1945 Conference of the American States in Mexico City, the Act of Chapultepec was adopted which declared that an attack on any American state would be considered as an attack against all and that collective measures would be taken to repel the aggression. The Conference decided that the Inter-American Defence Board, established in 1942, should be made a permanent organization. It also recommended a permanent unified military command of the 21 republics including the standardization of equipment, training and organization. This resulted on September 2, 1947 in a military pact, the 'International Treaty of Reciprocal Assistance' known as the Rio Pact which would provide for "collective self-defence" and would "tend to serve as a guarantee to peace in the Americas."

In March-May 1948, the Ninth International Conference of American States at Bogota drew up the Charter of the Organization of American States (OAS), highlighting the necessity for increasing hemispheric solidarity in political, economic and military matters.

The Caracas Declaration of 1954 stated that:

> The domination or control of the political institution of any American state by the international Communist movement extending to this hemisphere the political system of an extra-continental power, would constitute a threat to the sovereignty and political independence of the American states, endangering the peace of America, and would call for a meeting of consultation to consider the adoption of appropriate action in accordance with existing treaties. [4]

Military aid was stepped up for the oligarchy in the Caribbean and Latin America on the argument that every country should co-operate in meeting the so-called communist threat. It was argued that it was the responsibility of all the states to protect the strategic areas of the hemisphere and the Inter-American lines of communication as these were vital for the security of every American Republic.

Bilateral military treaties were signed with several Latin American and Caribbean States, reducing them virtually to client-states of the USA. Such was their vassal status that US laws - the

Law of Reciprocal Aid of 1949 and the Law of Mutual Security of 1951 - were also applicable to them. Under the first Mutual Defence Association (MDA) agreement between Ecuador and the USA in January 1952, Ecuador agreed "to facilitate the production and transfer ... of ... strategic materials required by the United States" and to co-operate in the blocking of trade with the socialist world; the United States government agreed "to make available ... equipment, material, services and other military assistance designed to promote the defence and maintain the peace of the Western Hemisphere".[5]

In return for military aid, the United States obtained military bases. Apart from those previously established at Guantanamo in Cuba and the Canal Zone in Panama, missile-tracking stations were set up in the Dominican Republic and Fernando de Noronha Island. In 1958, the United States established its Military Forces Southern Command in the Panama Canal Zone to monitor the situation in Latin America. Also located in this zone was the Special Action Force in Latin America designed for emergency situations.

The military build-up could not be justified on any ground except to maintain and strengthen the triarchy - the military, the landlords and the high clergy - a tiny privileged group, traditionally associated with feudalism and backwardness. It led to the ouster of several popular democratic regimes. Before the mutual security pact was launched in 1947 at the Rio Conference, only three nations - Argentina, Nicaragua and the Dominican Republic - were dictatorships. But by 1953 military men, who had taken the anti-Communist pledge, had been given arms and equipment and had ousted the legal governments in seven other republics. From 1948 to 1958, there were 14 major coups d'etats.

The Venezuelan government of Romulo Gallegos, the renowned patriot and novelist, was overthrown in 1948 by three colonels headed by Colonel Marcos Perez Jimenez. In 1949, Laureano Gomes established a Franco-type dictatorship in Colombia. In 1954, the Arbenz government in Guatemala was overthrown by Colonel Armas with the help of the Central Intelligence Agency. In 1953, the British Government forcibly removed the popularly elected government of the People's Progressive Party (PPP) in British Guiana.

THE PRINCIPLES AND GOALS OF NAM

Against the background of the cold war, and based on their own experience of colonialism, neo-colonialism, imperialism and racism, India, Indonesia, Burma and Egypt were not willing to become members of the Western multilateral military pacts, and to be associated with the policy of atomic bomb rattling which could lead from a limited nuclear war to a global holocaust. They saw the need for a non-aligned position for the purpose of improving the world political climate and utilising manpower and other resources for development, economic emancipation and social progress.

The concept of Non-Alignment originated in India, and "took root in the halls of United Nations in 1946 and 1947."[6] Jawaharlal Nehru, regarded as the father of Non-Alignment, played a decisive moral/political role in the post-war period, filling the vacuum created by the death of President F D Roosevelt and the failure of his successor President Harry Truman to continue his predecessor's 'New Deal' policy at home, 'Good Neighbour' policy in Latin America and mediator role between Winston Churchill and Josef Stalin during World War II. As the then leader of the Interim National Government, he declared on December 7, 1946:

> We propose, as far as possible, to keep away from the power politics of groups, aligned against one another, which have led in the past to world wars and which may again lead to disasters on an even vaster scale ... we shall take part in international conferences as a free nation with our own policy and not as a satellite of another nation.[7]

Nehru made it clear that Non-Alignment did not mean neutrality; that it had a negative as well as a positive aspect - negative, in the sense of not being aligned with any military blocs, but as he put it, "this in itself is not a policy, it is only part of a policy", and positive in the sense of concern for peace and socio-economic development. This was spelt out by him in a speech at Columbia University on October 17, 1949 when he described the totality of India's foreign policy:

> The pursuit of peace, not through alignment with any major power or groups of powers but through an independent approach to each controversial or disputed issue, the liberation of subject peoples, the maintenance of freedom, both national and individual, the elimination of racial discrimination, elimination of want, disease and ignorance which afflict the great part of the world's population.[8]

The Colombo Powers (India, Ceylon, Pakistan, Burma and Indonesia) took the initiative in convening the Afro-Asian Conference at Bandung, Indonesia in April 1955. The 29 states, though holding different position (8 - non-aligned; 2 - socialist; 19 - pro-West) unanimously adopted a Declaration on the Promotion of World Peace and Co-operation, a set of 10 basic principles. These included the five principles of peace for Panch Shila, which had been inserted in the preamble of the Tibet Agreement of June 24, 1954 between India and China:[9]

> a) Mutual respect for each other's territorial integrity and sovereignty;
> b) Non-aggression;
> c) Non-interference in each other's internal affairs;
> d) Equality and mutual benefit;
> e) Peaceful co-existence.

The other five points included a stand for national freedom and against colonialism and racial discrimination; for the prohibition of nuclear and thermonuclear weapons; for economic and cultural co-operation of the nations of Asia and Africa; and on specific questions affecting West Asia, Palestine, Aden and the North African nations. These became the guiding principles of, and provided the framework for, the first Non-Aligned Summit Conference in Belgrade in 1961, and subsequent meetings.

In the context of the Bay of Pigs invasion of Cuba organised by the Central Intelligence Agency, the threat of a nuclear conflict and the calling-off of the 2nd Summit Conference of the Big Powers as a result of the American U2 spy plane incident over Soviet territory, the first Non-Aligned Conference in Belgrade in 1961 sought to play a mediatory role in defusing conflict. In keeping with the spirit of Bandung, it considered that "the principles of peaceful co-existence are the only alternative to the 'cold war' and to a possible general nuclear catastrophe"; further, that peoples and governments "shall refrain from the use of ideologies for the purpose of waging the cold war, exercising pressure of imposing their will."[10] The Conference proclaimed that the Non-Aligned countries did not wish to form a new bloc and could not be a bloc. The participants solemnly reaffirmed their support to the "Declaration on the granting of Independence to Colonial Countries and Peoples," adopted at the 15th Session of the General Assembly of the United Nations, which recommended "the immediate, unconditional, total and final abolition of colonialism" and resolved "to make a concerted effort to put an end to all types of new colonialism and imperialist domination in all its forms and manifestations."[11] The Belgrade Summit also condemned the policy of apartheid practised by the Union of South Africa, demanded the immediate abandonment of this policy, and declared that the policy of racial discrimination anywhere in the world constituted a grave violation of the Charter of the United Nations and the Universal Declaration of Human Rights. The participants reaffirmed their conviction that:

a) all nations have the rights of unity, self-determination, and independence by virtue of which rights they can determine their political status and freely pursue their economic, social and cultural development without intimidation or hindrance,

b) all peoples may, for their own ends, freely dispose of their natural wealth and resources without prejudice to any obligations arising out of international economic co-operation, based upon the principle of mutual benefit and international law. In no case may a people be deprived of their own means of subsistence.

The Conference pointed out that the presence of a military base at Guantanamo, Cuba, against the wishes of the Government and people of Cuba, affected the sovereignty and territorial integrity of that country. It also called on those countries which recognised the People's Republic of China to recommend that the General Assembly should accept the representatives of the Government of the People's Republic of China as the only legitimate representatives of that country in the United Nations.

In the wake of developments in the then Belgian Congo and the intrigues against the government led by Patrice Lumumba, his incarceration and subsequent murder, the Cairo Summit in 1964 was mainly concerned with the problems of colonization. It convened at a time when the Moscow Treaty on the prohibition of above-ground testing of nuclear weapons was being signed. Its Declaration proposed a Programme for Peace and International Co-operation and concerted action for the liberation of countries still dependent, through the elimination of colonialism, neo-colonialism and imperialism. It called for the codification of the Principles for Peaceful Co-Existence by the United Nations, the settlement of disputes without threat or use of force in accordance with the Principles of the United Nations Charter, respect for the sovereignty of states and their territorial integrity, general and complete disarmament, peaceful use of atomic energy, prohibition of all nuclear weapons test, establishment of nuclear free zones, prevention of dissemination of nuclear weapons, abolition of all nuclear weapons and for the diversion of resources then employed on armaments to the development of under-developed parts of the world for the promotion of the prosperity of mankind.[12]

The Conference welcomed the establishment of the Organization of African Unity (OAU) as an important contribution to the strengthening of world peace and called for the co-ordination of the efforts of the Non-Aligned Movement and the OAU with a view to safeguarding their joint interest in economic, social and cultural development and in international co-operation.

The Lusaka Conference in 1970 issued a Declaration on Peace, Independence, Development, Co-operation and Democratisation of International Relations. Held in the context of sharpening liberation struggles in Africa and Vietnam, economic deterioration and the failure of the UN First Development Decade to narrow the ever-widening gap between the developed capitalist states and the imperialist-dominated underdeveloped countries, it concentrated on liberation questions and economic issues.

The participants pledged:

(a) to cultivate the spirit of self-reliance and to this end to adopt a firm policy of organizing their own socio-economic progress and to raise it to the level of a priority action programme, and

(b) to exercise fully their right and fulfil their duty so as to secure optimal utilisation of the natural resources in their territories and in adjacent seas for the development and welfare of their peoples.

The Conference made a forceful statement about the right of the Indochinese peoples to self-determination, and called for effective material aid for national liberation movements. Calling for firmness and action, it noted: "What is needed is not redefinition of non-alignment but a rededication by all Non-

Aligned nations to its central aims and objectives."[13]

The Non-Aligned Meeting of Foreign Ministers in Guyana in 1972 took decisions which were an important landmark in the history of the Movement. The Royal Government of the National Union of Cambodia in exile and the National Liberation Front of South Vietnam were seated. This caused Indonesia, Laos and Malaysia to walk out of the Conference in protest. In a decisive way, the NAM gave notice that, standing firm on fundamental principles, it would act forthrightly on behalf of national liberation, and would not submit to the whims and fancies of puppet regimes which had been put in power with the help and connivance of imperialism.

The Algiers Summit in 1973 was held under more favourable international conditions; sections of the ruling class in the United States had accepted the policy of peaceful co-existence, which ushered in a period of detente, the weakening of anti-communist hysteria and relaxation of tensions. Against the background of recession in the capitalist world and growing difficulties in the developing countries, the Algiers Conference put special emphasis on economic questions, which led to the demand for a New International Economic Order and just and equitable economic relations.

The Colombo Summit Conference in 1976 was attended by over 80 nations in the context of a fluid international situation. The Helsinki Accords of 1975 ushered in a period of political detente in Europe and confrontation in Angola. Reactionary regimes had been removed in Greece, Ethiopia, Portugal and its colonies in Africa. This was paralleled by the establishment of fascist regimes in Chile and elsewhere in Latin America. The Conference placed special emphasis on collective self-reliance, namely, economic co-operation among non-aligned and other developing countries, and special attention to the question of non-interference in internal affairs of states.

Concerned with the worsening international situation, the decision by the NATO powers to increase their military expenditures, and the formidable, particularly mounting debt problems facing the underdeveloped countries, the Havana Summit in 1979 laid special stress on the related problems of peace, disarmament and development - political dentente to lead to military detente; disarmament to lead to the substantial transfer of resources for the solution to the problems of underdevelopment, hunger, malnutrition, illiteracy and disease.

USSR, USA AND THE NAM

As a national liberation, and thus objectively a profoundly anti-imperialist movement, the main goals of Non-Alignment received the understanding and support of the Soviet Union and other socialist countries.

At the 1947 Conference in New Delhi of representatives of 27 Asian countries called by Jawaharlal Nehru, the first attempt at collective action included public figures from the Soviet Central Asian and Caucasian Republics, the Mongolian People's Republic and the Democratic Republic of Vietnam; and the Bandung Conference included the Democratic Republic of Vietnam and the People's Republic of China.

The 20th Congress of the Communist Party of the Soviet Union welcomed the Bandung Conference as representing "the best formula for relations between countries with different social systems under present circumstances and would serve as the basis for stable peaceful relations between all countries of the world."[14]

After the Algiers Summit Conference (1973) emphasised that the Non-Aligned countries should fight together with other progressive forces for democratisation of international relations, world peace and equality between states, President Leonid Brezhnev of the USSR pointed out that "there is no doubt that such a position and its consistent implementation will be conducive to the further growth of the non-aligned countries' influence in the world arena. For our part, we have every respect for the anti-imperialist programme drawn up in Algiers, and we wish the participants of the movement of non-aligned countries success in putting it into effect."[15]

The USA, particularly furious that its allies, chiefly Malaysia and Ceylon, did not succeed in their orations about "communist imperialism" and "communist aggression" to turn Bandung from a anti-imperialist into an anti-communist Conference, denounced the concept of Non-Alignment. John Forster Dulles, US Secretary of State, on June 9, 1955, stated that US mutual assistance treaties:

> with forty-two countries of America, Europe and Asia... abolish as between the parties the principle of neutrality, which pretends that a nation can best gain safety from itself by being indifferent to the fate of others. This has increasingly become an obsolete conception and, except under very exceptional circumstances, it is an immoral and short-sighted conception.[16]

Vice-President Richard Nixon on July 5 also condemned it and warned against the "brand of neutralism that makes no moral distinction between the Communist world and free world. With this viewpoint, we have no sympathy."[17] In other words, the US government's position was blunt: if you are not with us, you are against us. Non-Aligned states were thus treated as enemies, at best semi-enemies. The United States not only did not take part in the Geneva Conference on Vietnam in the summer of 1954, but also did not respect the decisions of the Conference for a Non-Aligned Laos and Cambodia (now Kampuchea) and for elections in 1956 to unite North and South Vietnam. In fact, the CIA engineered the overthrow of the Sihanouk Non-Aligned government of Cambodia and escalated the war in Indochina.

With the Cuban revolution and other revolutionary successes in Asia and Africa, imperialism reacted with a carrot-and-club policy, and more flexible and subtle tactics. John F Kennedy, as Senator, "had come to object to the Dulles doctrine both as morally self-righteous and as politically self-defeating."[18] His reformist Alliance for Progress, introduced as a counter to the Cuban revolution, replaced the Puerto Rican model of development (Operation Bootstrap) and 'Point Four' Aid Programme for an "intermediary war of development" and a US-style neutralism, democratic in form but pro-imperialist in intent. He was prepared to support India's first five year plan. "We want India to win that race with China," he said, "... If China succeeds and India fails, the economic-development balance of power will shift against us."[19] He supported change, but provided it was kept within the bounds of the West's capitalist-imperialist system.

After the failure of the Bay of Pigs invasion of Cuba in 1961, US imperialism resorted to brinkmanship and diktat during the 1962 missile crisis. Anti-communist and anti-Soviet hysteria again became a big factor of international life, particularly after the assassination of President Kennedy.

President Lyndon Johnson, calling for the replacement of geographical frontiers "by ideological frontiers" for the preservation of freedom and democracy, the euphemism for capitalism/imperialism, proposed the grouping of Third World and Non-Aligned countries into regional alliances (Free Trade Areas and Common Markets) under the control of imperialism and the transnational monopolies. After US military intervention in the Dominican Republic in 1965, the Johnson doctrine (President Lyndon Johnson) reserved to the United States the right to intervene in any country perceived to be "threatened by communism." Under the doctrine, later supplemented by Richard Nixon's Guam doctrine and Gerald Ford's concept of maintaining an American intervention, and with a policy of "no more Cubas in the Western hemisphere," several Non-Aligned countries were destabilised.

President Jimmy Carter, like President John Kennedy adopted a more flexible approach. With his "ideological pluralism,"[20] he attempted to influence some of the Non-Aligned countries, like India and Jamaica under social-democratic Michael Manley, away from their anti-imperialist orientation. Soon after his inauguration, his wife Rosalyn Carter and later his Ambassador to the United Nations Andrew Young included Jamaica in their

Latin American and Caribbean goodwill tours, shortly after Prime Minister Michael Manley had survived a CIA destabilisation attempt on his government in 1976.

According to Dr Z Brezezinski, Carter's National Security Advisor, in the context of "a rising crescendo of political and social demands" in the developing countries, "the Carter doctrine is based on the perceived need to try to get along with these forces rather than collide with them - and to channel them in a positive direction if possible.[21] What this meant was spelt out in *US News of the World Report* on January 9, 1978, when it stated that in India President Carter's objective "was to reinforce the Government's shift away from heavy reliance on the Soviet Union towards a more pro-US style of neutrality."

During the last days of the Carter administration and moreso under the Reagan administration, Washington shifted its position towards the Non-Aligned movement back to the days of John Foster Dulles.

ATTEMPTS TO DISRUPT THE NAM

The Imperialists and their clients consistently tried to disrupt the Movement. At the very beginning at the Bandung Conference in 1955, President Romulo of the Philippines charged that "communist imperialism is worse than capitalist imperialism." Some have charged that, with decolonization almost complete, "excessive radicalism" should be avoided in order to prevent disruption and even the crippling of the movement.

The charge was spurious. Political independence was meaningless without economic emancipation and progress toward a New International Economic Order. Neo-colonialism, which had supplanted colonialism, was "a great impediment to independent action," said former Foreign Minister of India, Swaran Singh in 1972, "and one of the principal tasks before Non-Aligned countries today must be to reinforce their efforts to arrest and eliminate its cancerous growth."[22]

At the 1970 Lusaka Non-Aligned Summit, which made a forceful statement about the right of the Indochinese peoples to self-determination and called on Third World governments to provide effective material aid for national liberation movements, the then Cuban Foreign minister Raul Roa declared:

> Our concept of Non-Alignment is established in these words. For Cuba, the keystone of Non-Alignment is the attitude to be adopted in the face of imperialism, the real and sole source of the poverty, injustice, discrimination, scorn, backwardness, brutality and aggression we denounce and combat.[23]

Maoist China also sought to divide the Non-Aligned movement and to isolate it from the Soviet Union and other socialist countries. After creating border incidents with Non-Aligned India and a breach of relations with the Soviet Union, it attempted at the second Intergovernmental Conference of Asian and African countries (Bandung II) to create a pro-Chinese and anti-Soviet bloc of Afro-Asian states. Later, it called the 1966 Delhi Meeting of the three top Non-Aligned leaders - the Presidents of Egypt and Yugoslavia and the Prime Minister of India - "a new Munich of the East," a "big dirty deal on Vietnam," "part of the American-Soviet conspiracy." During the same period, it attacked the Soviet Union for its adherence to the policy of peaceful co-existence, deeming it a betrayal of the national liberation revolution. Later, after the failure of the cultural revolution, and its brazen attempts to make headway in the developing countries, it changed its tactics, once again accepting peaceful co-existence in order to influence the Non-Aligned countries to a position of anti-Sovietism. With the Maoist concept of 'three worlds,' Peking advised the Non-Aligned and developing countries ('the Third World') to join with the 'Second World' - the imperialist countries of the West, excluding the United States - in order to fight the two super-powers ('the First World'). However, since Peking was at the same time urging 'the Second World' to strengthen its ties with the United States within NATO, quite obviously, the whole affair took on an exclusively anti-Soviet appearance.[24]

Debunking the Maoist line, President Fidel Castro told the 1973 Algiers Non-Aligned Summit:

> There has been talk at this Conference of the different ways of dividing the world. To our way of thinking, the world is divided into capitalist and socialist countries, imperialist and neocolonialised countries, colonialist and colonialised countries, reactionary and progressive countries - governments, in a word, that back imperialism, colonialism, neocolonialism and racism, and governments that oppose imperialism, colonialism, neo-colonialism and racism.[25]

Answering the Maoist propaganda about Soviet 'great power hegemony' and 'Soviet Social-imperialism,' he went on to say:" How can the Soviet Union be labelled Imperialist? Where are its monopoly corporations? Where is its participation in the multinational companies? What factories, what mines, what oilfields does it own in the underdeveloped world? What worker is exploited in any country of Asia, Africa or Latin American by Soviet capital?" He proceeded to point out that the Soviet people from the days of the Great October Socialist Revolution had been rendering valiant service to the cause of anti-imperialism and liberation: "Not for a moment can we forget that the guns with which Cuba crushed the Playa Giron mercenaries and defended itself from the United States; the arms in the hands of the Arab peoples, with which they withstand imperialist aggression; those used by the African patriots against Portuguese colonialism; and those taken up by the Vietnamese in their heroic, extraordinary and victorious struggle came from the socialist countries, especially from the Soviet Union."[26] Hitting out at the splitters, he pointed out that the quality and not the number of members was what was most important if the movement was to wield moral and political power before the peoples of the world.

Attempts were made to expel Cuba and Vietnam from the

NAM on the ground that they were not Non-Aligned. Cuba was accused of interfering in Africa by sending military forces to Ethiopia and Angola. Said Barre of Somalia told an OAU meeting that "serious collective measures" should be considered to contain the "Cuban threat" in Africa.[27] Barre's Somalia, like Egypt and Sudan, had broken their friendship treaties with the Soviet Union and were being used by imperialism to disrupt the NAM.

Cuba answered these attacks by stating categorically that in so far as being a member of a multilateral military alliance she was Non-Aligned, but in so far as fighting for the key issues for independence, justice, progress and development which are of decisive importance for the entire struggle for world peace and the consolidation of detente, she was definitely Aligned.

Actually, the criterion for membership in the movement was that a Non-Aligned state was not part of a multilateral military alliance, and that its territory was not used as a military base by a foreign power. This did not mean, however, that a sovereign Non-Aligned country lost its inherent right of individual and collective defence, the right of defending its own territory either alone or with the assistance of other states when its own security and territorial integrity are endangered. The Non-Aligned Summit at Belgrade in 1961 in its Declaration had stated inter alia that support must be given to the "people fighting for their right to self-determination and concerted effort to end all varieties of neo-colonialist and imperialist domination."[28]

In recognition of this principle of lending support for the purpose of national liberation, President Fidel Castro, with reference to economic emancipation told the Non-Aligned Summit in 1973 in Algeria that "the true strength and profundity of the movement of Non-Aligned nations will be measured by the firmness of our actions regarding these problems. Cuba will back with the greatest determination the agreements adopted to that effect even if to do so calls for contribution of our blood."[29]

Later an attempt was made to shift the venue of the Sixth Non-Aligned Summit from Havana, Cuba, but it also failed. Thereafter, the United States sought to strengthen the hands of the rightists during the course of the Conference by declaring that there was a Soviet Combat Brigade in Cuba. This was intended to denigrate Cuba, to move the Non-Aligned movement to a US type of neutrality and a position of 'equidistance' - keeping an equal distance from the super-powers - thus isolating the Non-Aligned movement from the socialist world. Cuba and the Soviet Union denounced the alleged Soviet Combat Brigade as a lie. The Conference reaffirmed commitment of the participants to the principles and goals of the Non-Aligned movement.

THE NAM AND REACTIVATION OF THE COLD WAR

As in the post-World War II period and in the late 1950's, the latter part of the 1970-80 decade saw a decisive shift in the world balance of forces against imperialism. With the defeat of the United States and its allies in Indo-China, Vietnam was re-united and socialist states emerged in Laos, Kampuchea and Vietnam. The fascists and reactionaries were defeated in Guinea Bissau, Cape Verde, Mozambique and Angola. Dictatorial regimes were ousted in Iran and Afghanistan. A political settlement led to the removal of the fascist Ian Smith in Zimbabwe. In the Caribbean Basin, progressive forces won electoral victories in St Lucia, Curacao and Aruba. A mass upsurge brought down the hated Patrick John regime in Dominica. The dictators in Grenada and Nicaragua were overthrown. And in Suriname, progressive non-commissioned military personnel seized power.

The 'hawks' became furious; they went on the warpath. A month after the Saur Revolution in Afghanistan in April 1978, the NATO Council Meeting in Washington agreed on increasing military budgets of all member-states by three per cent per year until the end of the century.

Like her arch-conservative predecessor Winston Churchill, the 'Iron Lady' Prime Minister Margaret Thatcher, visited the United States and called for a 'get tough' policy. Her Conservative government severely reduced social welfare spending and increased defence expenditure to counter the supposedly increasing 'Soviet threat'. She argued that Britain and the West must talk from a 'position of strength.'

President Jimmy Carter, whose electoral fortunes had reached an all-time low, fell in line with the 'hawks' and the military-industrial complex. To induce the reluctant senators to ratify SALT II, he promised billions for the modernisation of US nuclear forces and a general programme for strengthening the 'Rapid Deployment Force'[30] - a crack, well-equipped 200,000-man contingency 'quick reaction' corps - for the purpose of protecting American interests and ensuring an uninterrupted flow of Arab oil. Forecasting 'storms of conflict' in the 1980's and a growth of 'political instability' he proposed, contrary to past electoral promises to cut military spending, an increase of 5 % above the inflation rate for 1980 and 4.5% for each of the next five years.

The first excuse for undermining and sabotaging detente was the announcement of the so-called Soviet military combat unit in Cuba. However, it failed to divert the Non-Aligned Movement at its Summit Conference in Havana from its true goals after the Soviet and Cuban governments' terse reply that it was a training unit which had been stationed in Cuba for the previous 17 years, and President Carter's admission that the unit posed no threat to the security of the United States. Soviet assistance to Non-Aligned Afghanistan then became the ground for wielding the 'big stick' and resorting to 'gunboat diplomacy.' SALT II was derailed, the Moscow Olympics was boycotted and shipment of grain to the Soviet Union was halted.

But the main reason for re-activating the cold war was neither the Soviet unit in Cuba nor the events in Afghanistan. A long time before the Afghan crisis, Hugh Sidey in his article, 'The Shape of Things to Come', in TIME (December 17, 1979) wrote:

> ... the Iranian crisis shocked today's Washington into a new sense of reality... Pentagon spirit is on the rise... the military-industrial complex is in subterranean

motion. Within hours of the start of the crisis, men from Lockheed, makers of the giant C-54 troop and equipment airlifter, were in Secretary of Defence Harold Brown's office, reviewing the American capacity to move military forces around the world. And engineers and technicians from Boeing and McDonnell Douglas scurried to the Pentagon with the announcement of plans for a Marine Rapid Deployment Force. The current official vocabulary has to do with American bases abroad, overflight rights with friendly countries, aerial refuelling capacity. The adrenaline is flowing... There is a body of opinion that the world worked better before men took to mineral water.

In the Caribbean, about 2,000 marines equipped with combat aircraft and submarines stormed into the US base at Guantanamo Bay in Cuba; military manoeuvres were carried out in the Caribbean Sea; arms were promised to Barbados and for a Caribbean security force; a Caribbean Joint Task Force was established at Key West, Florida, to improve US "capability to monitor and respond rapidly to any attempted military encroachment in the region;" there was increased surveillance of Cuba; increased economic assistance was promised to thwart "social turmoil."

There was also an escalation around the world. According to TIME (October 29, 1979):

> At Grafenwohr, West Germany, a US tank battalion roared into combat exercises after having been flown in from Fort Hood, Texas, on a "no notice" emergency drill. At Florida's Eglin Air Force Base, 20,000 soldiers, sailors and airmen prepared to launch "bold Eagle 80," a 9-day manoeuvre to practice coming to the aid of an invaded ally. In the Indian Ocean, a US Navy 7-ship carrier task force joined up with a 5-ship Middle East force to show the flag.

On December 10, 1979, the North Atlantic Treaty Organization (NATO) decided to deploy in Western Europe nuclear delivery vehicles and about 600 medium-range Pershing-2 and Tomahawk cruise missiles. The excuse for upsetting the balance of military forces in Europe was "Soviet military superiority," a "Soviet menace." But this was denied by President Leonid Brezhnev. He pointed out that there had been no increase in military (nuclear) hardware in the previous 10 years, that the Soviet Union was not planning an attack on the West.

The Carter administration had two major policy objectives; to improve the over-all US military posture, and to influence patterns of global change. To influence the course of socio-political transformations and to shape "a rapidly changing world in ways that would be congenial to our interests and responsive to our values." US Security Adviser Zbigniew Brezezinski[31] urged not a regional but a differentiated country to country approach, "where they demonstrate independence from Moscow and willingness to contribute to overall regional stability, we should encourage them. Where they do not, we should isolate them."

This is similar to Henry Kissinger's directive[32] in January 1976 when he had told the Senate Foreign Relations Committee:

> The hostility of some of the Third World spokesmen and bloc voting have made constructive discussions in the UN forums between the industrial and developing world almost impossible. I have instructed each US Embassy that the factors by which we will measure the value which that government attaches to its relations with us will be its statements and its votes on that fairly limited number of issues which we indicate are of importance to us in international forums.

At that time, the USA was complaining about "bloc voting" and "automatic majority" at the United Nations, what Kissinger called "the tyranny of the majority," meaning the socialist countries and the progressive newly-emergent Non-Aligned states.

As regards "our interests," Aberlardo L Valdez, USAID's Assistant Administrator for Latin America and the Caribbean, told the Inter-American Affairs Sub-Committee of the US House Foreign Affairs Committee on February 1971:

> Our concern for Latin America and the Caribbean begins with our strong traditional ties of trade and investment. The region provides many of the resources most vital to our economy. It is our third largest market after Western Europe and Japan, purchasing $20 billion in US exports. Our direct private investment exceeds $27 billion, 82% of our investment in the entire developing world. It earns $4 billion a year.

Actually, the outflow of capital from Latin America and the Caribbean in the form of profits, interests, depreciation and other payments increased from $5.8 billion in 1975 to $17.9 billion in 1980. In that period, the total drain was $60 billion, far more than the amount of foreign investments.

The Caribbean was also strategically important for materials such as oil (Venezuela, Trinidad and Tobago) and bauxite (Jamaica, Guyana, Surinam, Haiti and Dominican Republic), and as a sea lane. As such it was deemed the 'fourth border', the political and strategic 'soft under-belly' or 'Achilles Heel' of the USA.

"Our values" were spelt out in November 1979 at the Miami Conference on the Caribbean by former US Under-Secretary of State and US Ambassador-at-Large, Philip C Habib as five principles - significant support for economic development, firm commitment to democratic practices and human rights, clear acceptance of ideological pluralism, unequivocal respect for national sovereignty, strong encouragement of regional co-operation and of an active Caribbean role in world affairs.

The Reagan administration has shifted US policy back to the worst days of the cold war. Its main ideologues and advisers have accused the Carter administration of being too soft with the socialist world, working for an "anxious accommodation" as "if we would prevent the political coloration of Latin America to red crimson by an American-prescribed tint of pale pink",[33] giving encouragement to socialism and changes in the Non-Aligned countries and of alienating traditional 'friends'with its human rights fervour, thus sacrificing US 'vital interest.'

It has adopted a 'get tough' and 'no appeasement' position of the Dulles era, and is toying with Dulles' ideas of 'preventative war', 'limited nuclear war', 'brinkmanship' and 'selective retaliation'. It has whipped up the so-called Soviet rearmament threat, and plans the manufacture of the Neutron Bomb and the MX missile system. Ostensibly, this is done to overcome 'Soviet superiority' and to catch up with the Soviet Union. It is also vigorously pursuing the policy of 'selective militarisation' of client states. US arms sales abroad increased from $8,300 million (US) in 1974 to over $10,000 million in 1978, and to nearly $25,000 million in 1981. And the CIA has been unleashed.[34]

Actually, what is unfolding is a global strategy of 'containment' and 'liberation' by the western powers, spearheaded by the USA. The aim is to enlarge areas of conflict in various parts of the world - South East Asia, the Middle East, Southern Africa, Latin America and the Caribbean - with the objective of undermining the independence, particularly of Non-Aligned countries which are pursuing an anti-imperialist, socialist-oriented course, and "of crushing liberation movements, which threaten to dislodge feudal or reactionary regimes and culminating in open confrontation with the Soviet Union and other socialist countries which might come to their aid. The US aim is to escalate conflict on all fronts and to bring about a situation where the power of the socialist world will be stretched to the limit and the Soviet Union, in particular, will be unable to match the concentration of weaponry which the imperialist powers are assembling against her."[35]

In the Far East, the United States has concluded a strategic tripartite USA - China-Japan alliance directed against Non-Aligned Kampuchea, Laos and Vietnam; Pakistan, a former member of SEATO, will get $3,500 million US military aid to harass Non-Aligned Afghanistan and India; Israel also in a 'strategic alliance' with the United States is attacking Syria, Iraq and Lebanon; Saudi Arabia, Qatar, the United Arab Emirates and Egypt, organized in the Arab War Industrial Organization, are being supplied with sophisticated weapons, including advanced radar planes (AWACS) to Saudi Arabia , to keep progressive Arab States like Libya in line; Somalia has been compromised for attacks against Ethiopia. In Southern Africa, South Africa is again emboldened to attack Angola; Namibia is to be granted independence but not under the South West Africa People's Organization (SWAPO).[36]

Cuba is regarded as an agent of "Soviet expansionism" and is deemed an exporter of terrorism in the Western hemisphere. The Caribbean, "America's crossroad and petroleum refining centre, is becoming a Marxist-Leninist lake," according to the Committee of Santa Fe. Non-Aligned Nicaragua and Grenada are considered tools of the Soviet Union and Cuba. Using the harshest anti-communist rhetoric reminiscent of the inflammatory speeches by Winston Churchill at Fulton, Missouri in 1946 and President Harry Truman at Baylor University in 1947, President Reagan in his address to the Organization of American States (OAS) in February 1981, declared that democratic governments were being threatened by a "new kind of colonialism" which "stalks the world today and threatens out independence. It is brutal and totalitarian." Invoking the Monroe Doctrine, he continued: "it is not of our hemisphere, but it threatens our hemisphere and has established footholds on American soil for the expansion of its colonialist ambitions."

The old fallacious 'falling dominoes' theory used in South East Asia has been revived: if El Salvador goes, Guatemala and Central America will go, and if Central America goes, US security will be threatened. Using the sabre-rattling language of the Johnson Doctrine, he said: "If we do not act promptly and decisively in defence of freedom, new Cubas will arise from the ruins of today's conflicts." He warned "that we will do whatever is prudent and necessary to ensure the peace and security of the

Caribbean area." He explicitly invoked the Rio Treaty of Reciprocal Assistance of 1947 and promised increased security assistance.

The US government has increased spending to $92.6 million in outright military aid for 21 Latin American countries in the October 1981 - October 1982 period: a 60 percent increase on the $58 million allocated by the Carter administration. Of this $28 million will be going to the junta in El Salvador, in addition to $25 million supplementary appropriation already granted to it. Now, additional military aid will be given to El Salvador to keep an oppressive and repressive military clique in power and to oppose the struggle for national liberation.

The United States is also giving what it calls 'Foreign Military Sales' (FMS) credits, and 'International Military Education and Training' (IMET) funds: the Bahamas will be getting more than $1 million, Barbados more than $2 million, Jamaica over $1 million, with smaller sums to Guyana, St Lucia, St Vincent and Surinam. In addition, $20 million is being made available to the Eastern Caribbean from what has been called an 'Economic Support Fund' (ESF).

Because of the explosive economic, social and political situation in the Caribbean and Central America, the United States has brought forward the Caribbean Basin Initiative (CBI). Prime Minister Edward Seaga of Jamaica had first mooted the idea by calling for a mini-Marshall plan; it was taken up by Chancellor Schmidt of West Germany. The main components, designed "to make use of the magic of the market of the Americas," are: US trade preference for products such as sugar and duty free importation into the USA for the next 12 years of labour-intensive manufactured goods, except textiles and apparel products, from the Caribbean countries; incentives to US companies to invest in the Caribbean; an 'aid' package of about $350 million (US); technical assistance and training and security ties. To qualify, the recipient countries will have to accept the basic philosophy behind the plan, must create an investment climate, pursue a capitalist course, and become integrated into the geo-political and strategic system and objectives of US imperialism.

The basic philosophy behind the CBI is that the Caribbean, like other Third World countries, must look to the private sector for economic development and create a climate attractive to investment and trade. In this regard, it is similar to the basic foreign economic tenets of the Truman Doctrine for the 'containment of communism'; the Marshall Plan and 'Point Four' aid programmes; the Puerto Rican 'Operation Bootstrap' model of economic development based on private foreign capital and the creation of an investment climate within the country; and bilateral MDA agreements.

The Reagan administration has shifted emphasis from aid to trade and private investment and from multi-lateral co-operation, and it has reduced financial allocation even to the international lending institutions like the International Monetary Fund, the World Bank, the Inter-American Bank, and others under its control. President Reagan told the World Affairs Council that "free people build free markets that ignite dynamic development for everyone." Investment, he declared, "is the life blood of development, and improving the climate for private investment" was one of his administration's major priorities.

The CBI has earmarked a sum of $350 million for economic aid[37] mostly concentrated on the private sector; also about $166 million for military aid to El Salvador next year. Of the economic aid package, $100 million and $120 million will go to bankrupt El Salvador and Costa Rica respectively, and most of the rest to Jamaica. Nicaragua and Grenada, deemed to be under "the tightening grip of the totalitarian left," along with Cuba are excluded. This is similar to aid with political strings under the Marshal Plan (1947), organized for American "economic-political intervention in Western Europe as a preliminary to its military organization NATO [constituted in 1949] under United States control."

According to President Reagan, "before granting duty-free

treatment, we will discuss with each country its own self-help resources," and "bilateral investment treaties will be negotiated."[38] This, like the old MDA agreements, will mean more "conditionality" (pressures) in addition to those already applied by US-controlled institutions like the International Monetary Fund (IMF) and the World Bank, which have wreaked havoc in countries like Peru, Jamaica and Guyana with respect to the economy and people's welfare. The aim is to create a pro-imperialist axis of Caribbean States armed to the teeth, possibly organized in a Regional Defence Force, to co-ordinate with the US Caribbean Joint Task Force, now upgraded to a Caribbean Command for 'mutual defence.' And to continue the programme of psychological warfare, intimidation and harassment, the biggest-ever NATO exercises will be carried out in March 1982 in the Caribbean.

Washington is implementing President Nixon's 'Vietnamisation' policy - reviving the idea of a so-called Inter-American Peace Force and a Caribbean Defence Force, instigating and utilising some Caribbean and Latin American countries to fight others, and supplying the arms. With Cuba principally in mind, Venezuela is purchasing 24 F16 supersonic fighters; it has also suspended diplomatic relations with Cuba. With the same objective of isolating Cuba, Columbia and Costa Rica, like Venezuela with NAM observer status, have been pressured to break off diplomatic relations. Although Cuba is the current Chairman of the Bureau of the Non-Aligned Movement, and was its spokesman through its President, Fidel Castro, at the 1979 UN General Assembly meeting, it was not permitted to take part at the Cancun Summit Meeting in Mexico, President Reagan insisted that United States would attend only if Cuba was excluded. Also excluded were Nicaragua and Grenada.

Costa Rica has also been forced to join with Honduras and El Salvador in the Central American Democratic Community to isolate Nicaragua; the same Costa Rica which had previously given sanctuary to the liberation fighters of Nicaragua, was actually a base for one of the sections of the Sandinista Front, and had joined with seven other Central and South American countries to oppose at at OAS meeting in 1979 US intervention in Nicaragua. The Reagan administration also suspended assistance to Nicaragua, on the pretext that it was supplying arms to the revolutionary forces in El Salvador. And Argentina is being pressured to play the role of US gendarme in El Salvador - a role previously played in the mid-1960's by Brazil as in the Dominican Republic in 1965.

Pressures put on the three signatories - Grenada,[39] Dominica and St Lucia - of the Grenada Declaration led to the split of the St Lucia Labour Party (SLP) and finally the fall of the SLP government, the replacement of the progressive Seraphine government of Dominica by the Eugenia Charles' conservative Freedom Party government, and a well-orchestrated local and foreign campaign of destabilization against Grenada. Washington also applied pressure on the IMF not to grant extended fund facility and compensatory financing facility of $19 million to Grenada, a Non-Aligned state, and on the EEC not to support its application for aid for its airport; blocked hurricane relief specifically to it and not to its neighbours in the Organization of Eastern Caribbean States; and demanded that no part of a US loan to the Caribbean Development Bank should be disbursed to it. The British Government also, while supplying armoured trawlers to Barbados and St Vincent, reneged on a promise to sell two armoured cars to Grenada

In the Western Caribbean, the United States has also concluded bilateral agreements with Haiti and the Dominican Republic. The two Caribbean countries agreed to render military assistance to each other in case of a serious revolutionary mass upsurge. The Pentagon has announced plans for spending $21 million in fiscal 1983 starting in October 1982 for the purpose of airfield improvements in the Caribbean region, which will guarantee "access to the airfields by US aircraft."

The countries, which are likely to become members of the pro-imperialist axis for the isolation of genuinely Non-Aligned

Cuba, Nicaragua and Grenada, are Honduras, Guatemala and El Salvador in Central America; Jamaica, Haiti, Dominican Republic, Antigua, Colombia, Venezuela, Barbados, Dominica, St Vincent and Guyana in the Caribbean.[40] The Prime Minister of Antigua recently remarked that the United States had the right and the duty to defend the Caribbean!

THE ROLE OF THE NAM

The Non-Aligned Movement has taken numerous initiatives internationally and regionally and made substantial gains. While it has not attained all its objectives, it has helped to bring down the political temperature, to reduce tensions which were likely to lead to confrontations among the Big Powers. By its efforts to soothe, to convey nuances and impressions, to act in the interstices of great power relations, it has served to preserve world peace, and thereby to become an indispensable political force. Its voice has been heard on important questions - the Korean war, the Suez crisis in 1956 and the Congo incidents in 1960-61, decolonization, disarmament and a New International Economic and Information Order. Recognizing political detente as "a detente based on mutual fear,"[41] it has struggled for military detente - disarmament and the creation of Peace Zones in the Indian Ocean and elsewhere. Its efforts in this direction led to the UN General Assembly adopting a resolution in favour of the suspension of nuclear tests in 1959,[42] and subsequently to the calling of a Special Session of nuclear tests in 1959,[43] and to the calling of a Special Session of the UN General Assembly devoted to Disarmament. The Initiative of Algeria, the then co-ordinating chairman of the NAM, led to the calling of the Sixth and Seventh Special Sessions of the UN General Assembly, which adopted the Declaration on the Establishment of a New International Economic Order and a Programme of Action.

Regionally, the Non-Alignment Movement, and in particular Cuba and Mexico, has made an invaluable contribution. The overthrow of the Batista dictatorship, in the context of other revolutionary, progressive and democratic developments in Asia, Africa, Latin America and the Caribbean, was an important landmark in the history of hemispheric affairs. The Cuban Revolution exploded the 'theory of geographic fatalism' and became an inspiration for the exploited and oppressed. Faced with threats and pressures, Cuba's socialist direction and participation as a member in the first Non-Aligned Conference in Belgrade in 1961 with three observers from national-democratic Latin American States (Brazil, Bolivia and Ecuador) was the first serious challenge to US imperialist hegemonism in the Western Hemisphere.

With the growth of the Movement from 25 members at the 1961 Belgrade Conference to over 100 members at the Havana Summit in 1979, Latin America and Caribbean participation steadily increased. At the Cairo Conference in 1964, the number of observers increased to nine. While the number of observers remained at nine, three other Caribbean countries joined Cuba to become full members at the Lusaka 1970 Summit Meeting; by 1979, there were 11 full members and 12 observers at the Havana Summit. This growth in membership and participation was a recognition of several factors:

> a) The importance of the Non-Aligned Movement in world affairs;
> b) The realisation by the progressive and revolutionary Latin American and Caribbean states, which came under all kinds of attacks and pressures - invasion, blockade and attempted isolation of Cuba, trade discrimination, conditional aid etc. - that there was a convergence between the Afro-Asian countries and themselves as to objectives and goals (the fight for peace and the struggle against a common enemy, imperialism), the attainment of which demanded united action on a world-wide scale.

This confluence was mutually advantageous and reciprocally influential - the participants from the region, long under the suffocating domination of foreign capital, the transnational corporations and the tyrannical local oligarchies, influenced the NAM positively; the NAM in turn acted as a shield against 'the colossus of the North' and from time to time took up vital issues pertaining to the welfare and security of the Caribbean and Latin American peoples.

The Belgrade Conference expressed the belief of the participating countries "that the right of Cuba as that of any other country to freely choose their political and social system in accordance with their own conditions, needs and possibilities should be respected"[44] The 1964 Conference in Cairo deplored the delay in the granting of independence to the Caribbean territories, including Puerto Rico in the light of Resolution 1514 (XV) of the United Nations. Section VIII of the Declaration adopted by the Conference urged the United States Government to negotiate with the Cuban Government for the evacuation of its military base at Guantanamo.

The Non-Aligned Foreign Ministers Conference held for the first time in the Western hemisphere in Guyana in 1972, reiterated the demand for a dismantling of all foreign military bases in different regions of the world, including Asia, Africa, Latin America and the Caribbean, particularly those established or maintained against the expressed wishes of the countries concerned. It expressed full support for the Chilean Government of President Salvador Allende, which it said, "is bent on consolidating its national independence and building a new society." Support was also pledged to the "nationalistic measures taken by the Peruvian Government and its efforts to safeguard the nation's sovereignty and to promote social progress." The participants commended the efforts of the people and government of Panama to "consolidate their territorial integrity," and generally welcomed the growth of the efforts being made by the Latin American peoples to recover their natural resources, reassert their sovereignty and defend the interests of their countries. The Conference further expressed full support for all governments which, "in the exercise of their sovereign rights over the natural resources of their countries have nationalised the interests of powerful foreign monopolies and restored them to their peoples in the interest of their welfare and national development."[45] It also adopted an Action Programme for Economic Co-operation, the Preamble of which stated, inter alia:

> The Ministers analysed in detail the results of UNCTAD III recently held in Santiago, Chile. While these showed once again the crisis international co-operation was experiencing, it was felt essential to continue to press for each of the proposals made by the Group of 77 in the Declaration of Lima. Accordingly, it was agreed to encourage its purposes. Attainment of the aims and objectives of the International Development strategy will depend on the concerted and consistent action of that Group...

The Non-Aligned Summit in Colombo in 1976, which accused imperialism, colonialism, neo-colonialism, Zionism and racism of hindering world development, detente and human progress, produced a Programme of Solidarity and Mutual Aid; denounced threats and new aggressions against Cuba made by United States imperialism; called on the members of the Non-Aligned movement to make every effort to speed up the Puerto Rican people's decolonization process and to offer them their solidarity and support in achieving self-determination and independence; welcomed the participation of Belize, whose aspirations for independence continue to be frustrated by territorial claims; reiterated its firm solidarity with the government and people of Panama in their fair struggle for their effective sovereignty with the Peruvian people and with the government of the armed forces of Peru in their valiant and just effort to consolidate and deepen the gains of the Peruvian revolution, to affirm their sovereignty and promote economic, political and social transformation for the benefit of their people; paid homage to the Latin American leader, Salvador Allende, and expressed its deep concern over the aggression and presence of imperialism in Chile, which was reflected in the reversal of the process of recuperating natural resources and making economic and social transformations in the country, in the flagrant violations of human rights there and the fact that the military junta had not allowed the United Nations Human Rights Commission to visit Chile. The Conference stated that the presence of United States military bases in Latin America, such as those existing in Cuba and Panama represented a threat to the peace and security of the region and renewed its demand that the government of the United States of America immediately restore to these countries the inalienable parts of their territories occupied against the will of their governments. The Conference also demanded the dismantling of the military bases that existed in Puerto Rico; backed and encouraged the nationalist and independent measure adopted during the period since the Fourth Summit Conference by Ecuador, Venezuela and Colombia, Panama, Mexico and other countries toward recuperating their natural resources and condemned every attempt at coercion or aggression such as the United States trade law passed by the United States Congress which particularly affected the Latin American countries, among others.[46]

The decision to hold the Sixth Non-Aligned Summit in Havana in 1979 was a means not only of lending support to the struggling peoples of the Caribbean and Latin America but also of paying tribute to Cuba for the achievements and historic role of its revolution: this socialist revolutionary base in the Americas had steadfastly adhered to the principles and objectives of the Non-Aligned movement. The successful outcome of the Havana Summit was also a great blow to the imperialists and their supporters within the movement. Recognising the necessity for unity, solidarity and action, Cuba, in 1966 hosted the Trio-Continental (Asian, Africa, Latin America and the Caribbean) Conference and a year later the Conference of Latin American Solidarity; it also set up in Havana the Tricontinental Organization, OSPAAL.

Mexico, with NAM observer status, played a progressive role in Caribbean affairs. It refused to join with five other Latin

American countries, under pressure from the USA and the OAS to sever diplomatic relations with Cuba. Non-Aligned Chile and Peru took a strong stand at the UNCTAD meeting in Santiago in 1971 against the transnational monopolies. This led firstly to the Economic Declaration against Transnationals at the Algiers Summit in 1973, which in turn led to a special UN conference on raw material resources in economic development; and secondly, to the formation of the Andean Pact - a regional economic grouping different from the previous imperialist-controlled Latin American Free Trade Association (LAFTA), Central American Common Market (CACM), and Caribbean Common Market (CARICOM) - which recognising that foreign capital and the transnational Corporation were the roots of the problems in Latin America, imposed certain restrictions.

In 1972, four Non-Aligned Caribbean countries jointly broke the OAS blockade and recognized Cuba. Non-Aligned Grenada took the initiative in 1979 for a tripartite (Grenada, St Lucia and Dominica) Caribbean unity, different from CARICOM, democratic and anti-imperialist in content. It also called for the Caribbean region to be declared a Zone of Peace. In the same year, eight states - the five Andean countries and Costa Rica, Mexico and Panama - blocked at an OAS meeting the United States from sending an interventionist force into Nicaragua.[47] This was a decisive victory, an historic turning point in hemispheric affairs.

New institutions and organizations have also been created to break out of the status quo. These include the Latin American Economic System (SELA); a regional Shipping Association (NAMUCAR); a regional Latin American and Caribbean Trade Union (CPUSTAL) to counter the CIA-controlled ORIT and AIFLD; a regional Trade Union Conference, first convened by the Central Council of Cuban Trade Unions, the Guyana Trades Union Congress and the Guyana Agricultural and General Workers Union in Guyana in 1977; the Latin American Federation of Journalists with headquarters in Mexico as a counter to the imperialist-controlled Inter-American Press Association, and a students' organization, OCLAE.

In the field of energy, Trinidad, Venezuela and Mexico came forward with their 'oil facility' schemes, intended to assist the region's energy problems. This came about particularly after Fidel Castro had criticised some of the OPEC countries for putting their surplus funds at the service of the imperialist nations and thus creating not only problems but divisions in the underdeveloped countries. On September 28, 1974 he had stated:

> If all the underdeveloped countries are to make the battle of petroleum theirs, it is imperative that the oil-producing countries make the battle of the underdeveloped countries theirs.[48]

In the context of the world capitalist recession, the worsening socio-economic situation in the Caribbean and Latin America, the aggravated situation in the Caribbean and Central America and the conditionality linked to the IMF, World Bank, Inter-American Bank and the Caribbean Basin Initiative, the Non-Aligned Movement is likely to suffer a setback in the immediate short-term period. Not all countries are willing to attune their foreign policies with the NAM principled goals which they subscribe to. Some in desperate need for budget and balance of payment support and with vacillating petty-bourgeois leadership, lack the political will to stand up to imperialist pressure and diktat.

Guyana is a classic example. During the past 17 years, the Burnham-led PNC government has moved, like a weather-cock, from a full-blown pro-imperialist to anti-imperialist and back again, now, to pro-imperialist, with in-between vacillation. The ruling Party's weak ideological understanding has permitted the US to get the required responses by playing in turn the siren's lyre or swinging a club. There is not space now to detail the sins of omissions of the regime in its domestic and foreign policies and Non-Aligned positions; it will suffice to say that it has led to both financial and moral bankruptcy. Colombia and Venezuela with NAM observer status have also somersaulted and, with seven other Caribbean and Latin American states, condemned Mexico and France for recognizing the FDR and the Farabundo Multi National Liberation Front as a representative political force and for calling for a negotiated settlement in El Salvador.

These and other setbacks, however, will only be temporary; they will not succeed in deterring the NAM from its goals. In this era of transition from capitalism to socialism, of sharpening national liberation and class struggles, of revolution, the people cannot be stopped. Imperialism, faced with any contradiction, will be defeated.

In the United States, as in other capitalist states, class battles in defence of living standards are sharpening. Faced with the threat of a new thermonuclear world war, the peace forces have become more assertive. In this regard, many of the allies in the Western Atlantic Alliance have expressed disagreement with the policies of the USA. Not as prostrate as in the immediate post World War II period, and unwilling to become the victims of a 'limited nuclear war' in Europe, several European allies of the United States have expressed opposition or reservations to the deployment in their territories of US nuclear missiles. Expressing the sentiments of millions of Europeans, William Borm, a veteran leader of the Free Democratic Party, the coalition partner with Helmut Schmidt's social-democratic Party in the West German government, demanded the establishment of a nuclear-free zone in Europe and increased conventional defence in an effort to escape 'capitulation or nuclear suicide.' NATO's nuclear doctrine, he charged, had led security policy into a dead-end street, and another war in Europe "would mean certain destruction for the Germans, East and West, but not so for the United States." He criticized the "adventurous ideas of some influential political circles in the United States," which have "the decision of life and death"[49] on German soil. Faced also with grave economic and serious unemployment problems, West Europeans are unwilling to sacrifice their national interests by terminating trade links with the socialist countries, which developed with the 'ostpolitik' policy of former Chancellor Willi

Brandt, and reverting to the old Cold War 'containment of communism' and trade embargoes.

Italy will not take part in the NATO manoeuvres near Cuba in March, 1982. Canada, like France in Europe, has exercised its independence and refused to carry out US diktat towards Cuba. It has decided to make its territory free of nuclear weapons, condemned the US decision to give additional military aid to the embattled El Salvador military junta, and like many other countries rejected the request to send observers to witness the farcical elections. The Sub-Committee on Canada's relations with Latin America and the Caribbean sharply criticised the Caribbean Basin Initiative as "poorly planned and questionably motivated." Mexico objected to the linking of aid to political-ideological yardsticks and objectives, and indicated that it should be open to all nations. Even close friends of the USA in the Caribbean are sceptical. Prime Minister Eugenia Charles of Dominica, who recently stopped all scholarships to Cuba, said that "private investment plays an important role in the modernization of developing countries, but we have more urgent needs." The Prime Minister of Barbados said that a Marshall-type Plan was irrelevant as a model for application to the developing world and rejected the idea that Caribbean development must be based solely on private initiative and the free market. He called for development as opposed to rehabilitation assistance, claiming that foreign investment "was being used as an excuse with no regard for the needs of the people."

Serious opposition has developed inside the United States against the economic philosophy at home and the interventionist policy of the Reagan administration in El Salvador. A recent public opinion poll showed opposition to the sending of US troops to that strife-torn country. The US Congress is moving to withdraw all military aid and advisers from El Salvador, and to curtail the President's present powers of committing US troops in foreign countries for 90 days in an emergency. The House of Representatives has already called for discussions between interested political forces in El Salvador.

Public pressure has forced the US State Department to explore the offer of Mexico to act as a mediator in the current conflict in Central America, and to normalise relations in the Caribbean Basin. This is a positive development and a recognition of the role of Non-Alignment as a viable alternative in the present geopolitical conjuncture and aggravated Caribbean situation.

Non-Alignment as a powerful voice however must not be confused with Non-Alignment as a third force: an equidistant force fighting against the two 'superpowers.' Non-Aligned Barbados and Guyana, unlike Cuba, Nicaragua and Grenada, have moved to this position.

Barbados Foreign Minister Louis Tull, addressing the UN General Assembly in late 1981, "called on Moscow and Washington to leave the Caribbean and Latin America to solve their own problems and to keep the area as a zone of peace."[50] He further pointed out:

> ..... it is with grave concern that we view the open competition of the two superpowers in this region. It is unfortunate and frightening that Moscow and Washington should choose the internal conflicts of Latin America and the Caribbean to extend their theatre of war. We reiterate our firm commitment to ensuring that the Caribbean should remain a Zone of peace. Barbados believes that the problems of Latin America and the Caribbean must be solved by the people of Latin America and the Caribbean.

This observation flies in the face of history, linking the oppressor with the oppressed, the exploiter with the exploited. Unlike the modern period of the USA, the whole history of the USSR is one of struggle for liberation inside and outside its territory. The assistance rendered to countries and peoples fighting for freedom and democracy has been attested to by many Non-Aligned leaders including Ahmed Sukarno, Kwame Nkrumah, Gamal Abdul Nasser, Indira Gandhi, Ho Chi Minh, Amilcar Cabral, Agostino Neto and Fidel Castro, to name a few. Aid from the socialist countries, especially the Soviet Union to

Non-Aligned and other 'Third World' countries has been decisive in the national liberation struggles in Ethiopia, Vietnam, Angola, Zimbabwe, Mozambique, Cuba, Guinea Bissau, Egypt (Suez crisis in 1956) and elsewhere, not only for securing and maintaining revolutionary-democratic people's power, but also for socio-economic transformations. Barbados, which refused to permit refuelling rights to Cuban planes bound for Angola in 1975, should be reminded that Angola could not have survived the military onslaught of South Africa and Zaire, backed by the CIA and China, had it not been for aid rendered by Cuba, the Soviet Union and other Socialist countries. This was why the Action Programme for Economic Co-operation, adopted by the 4th Non-Aligned Conference in Algeria included a special section on co-operation with the Socialist countries. It specifies that:

> the Non-Aligned countries shall encourage the development of scientific and technical co-operation with the socialist countries, inter alia, through the conclusions of inter governmental conventions, the establishment of the necessary joint bodies and the stimulation of relations between the organizations and institutions concerned.

Those who advocate an equidistant position and attack indiscriminately the two 'super-powers' must remember the fate of Dr M Mossadegh, Prime Minister of Iran, who after nationalising the Anglo-Iranian Oil Company had rejected co-operation with the Soviet Union - a tanker blockade strangled the country; his government was destablished by the CIA; he was placed under house arrest (where he subsequently died); the Shah returned and instituted a regime of torture and untold suffering for 25 years. Cuba did not make the same mistake as Iran under Mossadegh.

Vietnam also teaches important lessons. To meet the onslaught of an infuriated imperialism, it was necessary for her to develop the closest links not only with the socialist world, but also with the working class and democratic forces in the capitalist world and the national liberation movements in the 'Third World.' The people of the United States, for instance, played a significant role in forcing their government to bring an end to the undeclared but brutal war.

The Non-Aligned Movement will succeed to the extent that the individual countries translate into practical domestic and foreign policies the principles and goals of the movement; secondly, that economic goals are linked with the world political struggle for major objectives such as detente and disarmament; and thirdly, that the United Nations is strengthened to uphold the principles and objectives of its Charter, achieve disarmament, maintain world peace and pursue vigorously the 'Global Round' of negotiations for a New International Economic Order.

Above all, Non-Alignment must not become an ivory tower affair of governments. It will succeed only to the extent that in each country it becomes a genuine people's movement. This will ensure that the vacillating political leadership in some Non-Aligned countries are prevented from making an accommodation with imperialism against the people's vital interests. It will also a guarantee that the liberation movement will go forward to peace, freedom and social progress.

March 1982

[1] Paper published in *Journal of Caribbean Studies*, March 1982.

[2] D F Fleming, *The Cold War And its Origins* Doubleday & Company, Inc. New York, 1961, p.437.

[3] On February 10, 1952, John Foster Dulles, Foreign Policy Adviser to President Truman, in a broadcast stated: "the United States must not stand idly by while any part of the world remains under the rule of either communist or Fascist dictatorship" - cited in R Palme Dutt's *The Crisis of Britain and the British Empire* Lawrence and Wishart, London, 1957, p. 327.

[4] Santa Fe Committee, Council for Inter-American Security, Inc. *A New Inter-American Policy for the Eighties* New York, 1954, p.4.

[5] Edwin Lieuwen, *Arms and Politics in Latin America* Frederick Praeger, New York, 1960, p.4.

[6] C S Jha, *Non-Alignment in a Changing World* The Statesman Press, New Delhi, 1967, p.2.

[7] Ibid., p.5.

[8] C S Jha. op. cit., p. 4.

[9] R Palme Dutt, op. cit., p. 218.

[10] *Main Documents Related to Conferences of Non-Aligned Countries*, Ministry of Foreign Affairs, Guyana 1972, p.9.

[11] Ibid., p.10.

[12] *Main Documents Related to Conferences of Non-Aligned Countries* op. cit., p. 31.

[13] Ibid., p. 82.

[14] Ibid., p. 68.

[15] Nodari Simoniya, *Non-Alignment* Novosti Press Agency Publishing House, Moscow, p. 54.

[16] Ibid. p. 13.

[17] D F Fleming, op cit. p. 781.

[18] Ibid., p. 782.

[19] Arthur M Schlesinger Jr., *A Thousand Days: John F Kennedy in the White House* Andre Deutsch, London, p. 444.

[20] Ibid, p. 454.

[21] Nodari Simoniya, op.cit. p. 37 refers to the *Far Eastern Economic Review* (January 20, 1978, p. 16), which on the eve of President Carter's visit to India in January 1978, pointed out that "the US Government no longer feels as in the days when John Foster Dulles was Eisenhower's Secretary of State that to be neutral is immoral ... The watchword in Washington is that 'ideological pluralism' is understandable and acceptable in the emerging countries of the world." Similarly, for the countries of the African continent, President Carter wanted a new-colonialist alliance, like President Reagan's Central American Democratic community with Costa Rica, Honduras and El Salvador. He told *US News of the World Report* in June 1977: "If there is one overwhelming impression that's growing on me, it's the long-range strategic need - looking 10,15, 20 years in the future - for a close friendship and mutual trust, social and political alliance" (cited in *World Marxist Review*, March 1978, p. 18).

[22] Nodari Simoniya, op. cit. p. 37.

[23] *India News*, High Commission of India, Georgetown, Guyana, June 19, 1972.

[24] Nodari Simoniya, op. cit. p. 41.

[25] Ibid., p. 51.

[26] Fidel Castro, *The success and the future of the non-aligned movement will depend on its refusal to allow itself to be penetrated, confused, or deceived by imperialist ideology,* (Political Editions, Cuba, 1973), p. 12.

[27] Ibid., p. 14.

[28] *New Nation*, Guyana, August 6, 1978.

[29] Ibid.

[30] Fidel Castro, op. cit. p. 17.

[31] *US News & World Report*, February 27, 1978, p. 24.

[32] Zbigniew Brzezinski, *Foreign Affairs*, Spring 1979, p. 741, quoted in *International Affairs*, Moscow, January 1980.

[33] Ronald F. Dochsai, President of Council for Inter-American Security, in Foreword to *A New Inter-American Policy for the Eighties*, op. cit. p. Ii.

[34] R. S. Nyameko, 'Fight US subversion of Trade Union Movement in Africa' (*The African Communist*, No. 87, Fourth Quarter 1981) states "The CIA's experts on subversion confirm their role. William Colby, CIA Director under President Nixon, and Stansfield Turner, CIA Director under President Carter, stated: 'Covert action ought to be increased. The more aggressive the country's foreign policy, the more likely you are to use covert action as a supplement to diplomacy and as a substitute for military force."

[35] Ibid.

[36] Jeane Kirkpatrick told the Senate Sub-Committee on April 7, 1981: "I would desire a democratic Namibia with some sort of framework for stability, some sort of framework with autonomy, democratic Government. This solution is one broadly accepted not only by Namibia but its neighbours. In other words, an independent Namibia with a government acceptable to South Africa, and not a SWAPO government." - cited by R.S. Nyameko, op. cit p. 26. .

[37] Alistair McIntyre, former Secretary General of the Caribbean Common Market, in 1976 said that the region was faced with "unprecedented difficulties" including 20% inflation rate, a scandalous food importation bill of $1,000 million, a worsening balance of payments problem and the need for 150,000 jobs for full employment by the end of the 1970-80 decade. And he lamented the shortage of funds for the public sector and "startling increases" in consumption expenditure. William Demas, President of the Caribbean Development Bank, estimated that the employment rate was between 10% and 20% and for the 15 to 19 age group, it was as high as 50%. And the rate of labour underutilization was between 30% and 50% throughout the region. A group of 'wise men' appointed to diagnose the ills of the Caribbean territories pointed out that in the next decade, unless positive steps are taken to change the situation it would definitely worsen with the prospect for some countries of a 40% unemployment rate, which "would be nothing short of a catastrophe."

[38] Referring to the "Mutual Security Aid" programme under the Truman Doctrine. *The Times* of London on March 5, 1952 wrote: "The Programme will, as last year, be artificially divided into military and economic; and, as in 1951, there will be a tendency on the part of the Congress to accept the military part and cut the economic section to ribbons, because nobody understands that what is called economic aid is merely a cheaper form of military assistance." - cited by R. Palme Dutt, op. cit. p. 295. According to the *Guyana Chronicle* of March 2 1982, total US Security assistance is likely to increase by $1.67 billion for fiscal 1983 to $8.7 billion.

[39] The idea behind Central American Democratic Community is similar to the 'Betancourt Doctrine' of the late President Romulo Betancourt of Venezuela, a close friend of President Kennedy and the social-democratic Costa Rica leader Pepe Figueres - a doctrine which in the early 1960's condemned dictatorships of the right and the left. His proclamation that Venezuela would not recognize any government which did not come to power through the electoral process prepared the way for the diplomatic isolation and blockade of Cuba.

[40] *Guyana Chronicle*, March 5 1982, p. 9. In 1965, the Burnham-led coalition government, which was brought to power by Anglo-American imperialism, signed a secret agreement with the US government granting it the right to land military aircraft, equipment and personnel at Atkinson, now Timehri, airport; to build military installations; and to overfly Guyana territory. Egypt, Somalia and Oman have also provided similar facilities to the Pentagon.

[41] S Gopaul, 'Role of Non-Alignment in a Changing World,' *Indian Foreign Review*, May 15, 1976, p. 11.

[42] Ibid., p.12.

[43] C S Jha, op. cit., p. 8.

[44] *Main Documents Relating to Conferences of Non-Aligned Countries*, op. cit., p. 11.

[45] *Guyana Graphic*, August 15, 1972.

[46] *Sunday Chronicle*, August 12, 1976, p. 1.

[47] Similarly in Africa, the Non-Aligned front-line states in the Organization of African Unity achieved successes in Angola and Zimbabwe. In the latter country, for many years Britain kept in power the illegal Smith regime on the ground that it was not possible to use military force against 'kith and kin.' By 1979, on the threat by the African States at the Commonwealth Conference in Zambia to expel Britain from the Commonwealth, Prime Minister Margaret Thatcher, remarking that she was not prepared to draw African ire, agreed to a political settlement which led to the removal of Ian Smith and the assumption of power by Robert Mugabe.

[48] Fidel Castro, op. cit. p. 26.

[49] *Guyana Chronicle*, March 2, 1982.

[50] *Insight*, West Indian Committee, Goodyear Gibbs Ltd, London, November 1981, p.3.

Cheddi Jagan's 1953 Cabinet, including Sydney King, Janet Jagan and Forbes Burnham

Cheddi Jagan arrested in 1954 for breaking his restriction orders (restricting him to Georgetown after the suspension of the Constitution in 1953). He was subsequently imprisoned for six months

Cheddi Jagan leads PPP walkout of Parliament in the 1960s, in protest against PNC corruption

Cheddi Jagan leads protest against the Vietnam War, in front of the US Embassy in Georgetown in the 1970s. Jagan was President of the Guyana Peace Council

Cheddi Jagan addresses Parliament as leader of the opposition, speaking on the PNC rigging of elections in the 1970s

Cheddi Jagan meets the people of Linden, March 1994

Cheddi Jagan visits North West District to listen to people's views on education, with Ministers Nagamootoo and De Souza, and PPP General Secretary, Donald Ramotar, February 1996

Cheddi Jagan with Queh Queh dancers in celebration of his 78th birthday, State House, 24th March, 1994

Cheddi Jagan being sworn in as President of Guyana, 9th October, 1992, State House, Georgetown

Cheddi Jagan greeting street vendors and sellers at Christmas time, 1994

Cheddi Jagan opens new school for Amerindian children in the interior, December 1996

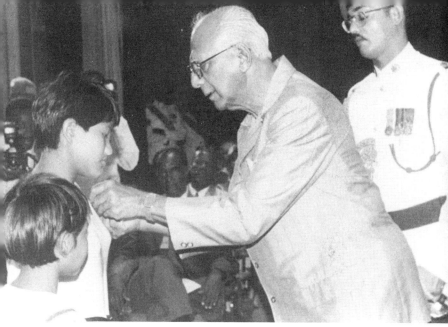

Cheddi Jagan presents national honours to two Amerindian sisters who survived after being lost in the jungle for 30 days

Cheddi Jagan meeting the people of Georgetown during one of his many city walks, 1994

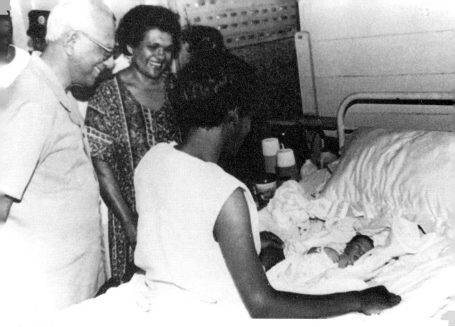

Cheddi Jagan speaking to mother of a new-born child, New Amsterdam Hospital, December 1995

Cheddi Jagan visits West Coast Demerara to discuss land distribution with villagers, 3rd August, 1995

CHAPTER THREE

THE CARIBBEAN IS REPELLING THE AGGRESSIVE COURSE

The aggravated situation in Central America and the Caribbean is not a product of intra-regional conflicts but rather of Washington's constant interference in the affairs of the Latin American people, its pressure on governments of the sub-region, and even direct military intervention.

President Reagan's May 9 1984 TV appearance once again showed the harsh outlines of the aggressive trend of US policy. Reagan described it as the United States' "lawful right and moral duty"[1] to suppress the revolutionary and national liberation movement of the region, indicating that Washington is continuing its line towards heightened international tension, new centres of armed conflicts and danger for universal peace.

The USA's adventurist course in Central America is fraught with tragic consequences for its people. An escalation of the dirty war against Sandinist Nicaragua is under way, as seen in the port mining, the attacks on fuel stores and the infiltration into its territory from neighbouring countries of Somocist armed mercenaries. El Salvador's ultra-right wing groupings, ill-famed for their genocidal crimes, are being encouraged. The dictatorial regimes in Guatemala and Honduras are receiving support. Tiny Grenada was cynically and brutally dealt with. Reagan's speech has placed the peoples of our republics even more on the alert and aroused their righteous indignation.

The situation in the region has its roots in complex socio-economic conditions that are being worsened by US imperialism's interference. Under its current president, the United States, in the role of international policeman, is not only occupying Grenada but also openly threatening other countries with war.

With the illegal invasion of Grenada, ostensibly to save lives and restore law and order and democracy, but in violation of the Charters of the United Nations and the Organization of American States, President Reagan brought US hemispheric policies back to the days of 'big stick' gunboat diplomacy when oceans of blood were shed, bringing suffering to the Latin American peoples. There is now a great danger that the conflict in Central America and the Caribbean could erupt into armed confrontation on a world-wide scale.

The USA wants to fill the 'vacuum'

Central America and the Caribbean Basin are marked by great diversity - a variety of state forms and economic and political structures. Territories with Colonial systems exist side by side with independent countries, be they constitutional monarchies or republics. The spectrum of political and administrative forms varies widely - socialist democracy, bourgeois-democratic parliamentarianism, neo-Bonapartism, bureaucratic military authoritarianism and rightist dictatorship. Some of these states are in military and political alliances, while others belong to the Non-Aligned Movement.

The post-independence period, particularly the past decade, has been very traumatic for the Caribbean economy. The 'vacuum' (as the White House called the situation in the Caribbean) created by the departure of the British was filled by US imperialism. In the first two years after the formation of the Caribbean Free Trade Association (CARIFTA),[2] the United States more than doubled its exports to the region. By 1978 the US was providing 86% of the capital flowing into the Caribbean.[3] Terence Todman, former US Assistant Secretary of State in the Carter Administration, highlighted the importance of the Caribbean: "The US economy has a very direct stake in the health of the economies of the Caribbean. We supply 35% of Caribbean imports and provide a market for 70% of the area's exports. In dollar terms this amounts to an annual trade exceeding US$6 billion."

Foreign domination and regional dependence on the US created serious problems for the Caribbean. In 1976, a summit meeting of the Caribbean Community[4] noted that the sub-region faced "unprecedented difficulties", including a 20% inflation rate, a "scandalous food importation bill of $1 billion and the need for 150,000 jobs to create full employment." The participants in the meeting would have liked to improve the situation, but it worsened in the 80's. A comprehensive report drawn up by the Caribbean Development Bank[5] reveals stagnation and gloom. The majority of countries are in the red, faced with serious balance of payments and foreign exchange difficulties. Export prices for regionally produced sugar and banana have reached an all-time low.

Guyana and Jamaica are now the most seriously affected. Their bauxite industries are particularly hard hit. A bauxite strategic stockpile deal[6] between the United States and Jamaica did not succeed in taking the country out of the economic doldrums. Indeed, the head of Reynolds Metal Company recently announced a complete shutdown of operations on the island.

Trinidad is facing serious economic problems with the drop in world oil prices, and its new multi-million dollar steel industry, on which high hopes were placed, was severely hit by US protectionist measures.

Through the International Monetary Fund (IMF), the World Bank and other institutions, imperialism is exerting pressure to get bourgeois prescriptions adopted for the grave social and economic crises, and to put the Caribbean countries firmly on a dependent capitalist course. On the one hand, the principal aim of the IMF is to ensure the non-interruption of the flow of hard currency, primarily in the form of debt and compensation payments, which have reached alarming proportions in Guyana[7] and Jamaica. On the other hand, the bourgeoisie and the ruling elites have no intention of giving up their privileges, extravagance and corruption. The end result of the so-called 'stabilisation' programme of the IMF is greater instability and growing problems for the overwhelming part of the Caribbean population.

Thus, the decolonization period has been marked by the seizure of the dominant positions in the sub-region's economy by US monopolies, which has undoubtedly been reflected in the character and content of the social and political processes developing there.

WHERE EVENTS ARE LEADING

The example of Cuba, Nicaragua and Grenada evidences the Caribbean people's considerable revolutionary potential. At the same time, many parties and groupings in the states of our zone are petty bourgeois and nationalist, with a Christian-democratic or social-democratic ideological orientation.

Political independence was given to the Caribbean countries when they were considered 'safe', the only exception being British Guiana (Guyana), where independence was delayed until 1966 after the People's Progressive Party (PPP) had been ousted from government. In the case of Grenada, the British ruling class hastily conferred independence in 1974, placing Eric Gairy[8] in power. In other words, independence created new nations but not new states. Under middle strata (local petty bourgeois) rule, the old administrative structure remained virtually intact under the conditions of neo-colonialism. The middle strata leadership had emerged in special circumstances under a slave and plantation system with a rigid social structure and colour bar. Race, colour, education and culture played their part in the formation of this strata's outlook and lifestyle. While distancing themselves from the working people, they at the same time found barriers to their social mobility into the ranks of the plantocracy. This developed into a kind of political schizophrenia with pragmatism/

opportunism on the one hand and radicalism on the other. This dual labour/capitalist tendency characteristic of the petty bourgeoisie led to political vacillation.

In the post-Depression and World War Two periods, the middle strata, having formed its own party groups and taken control of the trade union movement, played a positive role in the anti-colonial struggle for political independence. However, in the immediate post-war period, as a result of imperialist pressures and links with the right-wing social democracy of the developed capitalist powers, the Caribbean's political elite moved to the right. It adopted a conservative programme based on anti-communism, and failed to extend solidarity to the Guyanese and Guatemalan peoples when the popularly elected government of the PPP (British Guiana, 1953) and Jacobo Arbenz (Guatemala, 1954) became victims of imperialist ploys and direct aggression. The middle strata also adopted the Puerto Rican model of economic development based on 'industrialization by invitation' of foreign capital and the creation of 'a favourable investment climate'.[9]

With Washington leading the way throughout the 1960's the Caribbean states ostracised Cuba and other socialist countries in the diplomatic, economic, trade and cultural spheres. The only exception was British Guiana, which maintained ties with them up to 1964.

In the next decade, with the worsening economic and social situation and sharpening of the struggle, particularly in the favourable international climate of detente, and with the UN General Assembly call for a new international economic order and the developing countries' taking control of their natural resources, the radical tendency in the petty bourgeois's duality gained ascendancy. Where the middle strata were in power, they were forced to undertake some limited national tasks: 'localisation' (changing the personnel/management and share holding structures of the foreign-owned companies); 'partnership' (purchasing of shares by the state on a minority or, in some cases, majority shareholding basis in the foreign-owned companies); increased taxation of transnational corporations, as happened in Jamaica; and nationalization with generous compensation, as in Guyana.

Some Caribbean states also changed their foreign policy orientation somewhat during that period. The Trinidad and Tobago government took part in the Non-Aligned summit in Zambia in 1969. In Guyana in 1972, Cuba, Guyana, Jamaica and Trinidad and Tobago had delegate status and Barbados observer status at the second preparatory meeting of the foreign ministers of the Non-Aligned Movement. That same year, Jamaica, Barbados, Guyana and Trinidad and Tobago established diplomatic relations with Cuba. A close relationship developed between Cuba and these countries, particularly Jamaica and Guyana.

In the period of the reactivation of the cold war in the early 80's, the ruling groups of the majority of Caribbean states adopted a pragmatic, right-opportunist course in the face of an aggravated economic situation. They opted for handouts under Reagan's Caribbean Basin Initiative (CBI)[10] and have become linked in a political and military alliance with the United States. All the CARICOM countries, except revolutionary Grenada, lined up with Anglo-US imperialism during the Malvinas (Falklands) war.

In October 1982, St Vincent, St Lucia, Dominica and Antigua and Barbuda (revolutionary Grenada was excluded although she was a member of the Organization of Eastern Caribbean States) signed a Memorandum of Understanding for joint security operations. Prime Minister Vere Bird of Antigua and Barbuda said that the proposed regional security and military co-operation mechanism would be used to prevent "democratic governments" from being overthrown. He asserted that the region "cannot afford to have another Cuba or another Grenada",[11] and called for "a bigger and more active" US presence in the Caribbean to safeguard "democracy". For his own country, this has meant a US embassy,[12] two US military installations and a Voice of America 'booster' station.

The conciliatory pro-imperialist policy of the CARICOM member states' ruling circles meant that, within the exception of Trinidad and Tobago, Guyana, Bermuda and the Bahamas, they joined the United States in its criminal invasion of Grenada. Barbados, an active participant in the intervention, a country with a right-wing social-democratic regime led by Tom Adams, had assumed the role of "gendarme" of US imperialism in the Caribbean. In 1979, under the "Adams Doctrine" which stated that St Vincent and the Grenadines were within the security zone of Barbados, a contingent of police and troops was sent to quell a rebellion on Union Island. Two years later, the US financed an airlift of Barbadian troops to put down a revolt of a section of the army in Dominica. Such operations were fully in keeping with the traditional reactionary policy of the Barbados Labour Party in defence of colonialism and in opposition to the liberation struggle.

Supported by Dominica, the pro-imperialist Edward Seaga government of Jamaica is manoeuvring to create a new grouping of Caribbean states that would include Haiti and the Dominican Republic and be under the complete domination of US capital. In its turn, the ruling right-wing social-democratic party of the Dominican Republic has signed an agreement with the US on co-operation in fighting against the "communist threat". In particular, the Dominican armed forces are to aid the Duvalier dictatorship in Haiti should it come under attack by revolutionary patriots.

The Trinidad and Tobago government, with its petty bourgeois nationalist vacillations, neither aided the revolutionary process in, nor subverted, Grenada. This was in keeping with the ideological position adopted in 1956 by the ruling People's National Movement, which opted for "a middle way between the outright nationalization of Castro and the old-fashioned capitalist organization backed by the marines and the dollars of the United States of America".

In Guyana, the petty bourgeois nationalist (right-wing social-democratic, and since 1970, utopian "co-operative socialist") ruling People's National Congress (PNC) has established what it claims is a national estatist[13] regime. Nationalization of the foreign-owned sugar and bauxite industries has not served the people; their situation has even worsened and only a small section of the local bourgeoisie and the ruling elite (bureaucratic capitalist) has benefitted. In 1978, the government signed a very favourable agreement with the USSR: Guyana was to receive unlimited credit, aid to rehabilitate the bauxite industry and possibilities for bauxite sales, and assistance to develop the gold industry. However, instead of implementing the agreement, the PNC opted for an IMF course. Now, the PNC neither wants to retreat fully under pressure from Washington from the existing "co-operative capitalism" nor to advance with the PPP along the road of socialist orientation.

Unwilling and unable to carry out radical socio-economic transformations, the main Caribbean ruling groups are increasingly seeking to resolve growing problems, particularly unemployment, caused by dependence on the US, by expanding corrupt administrative and bureaucratic structures and intensifying political and racial discrimination. In the face of the sharpening national liberation and class struggles, the coercive bodies are being expanded and strengthened, notably the military and police (often called "security") apparatus.

The democratic and anti-imperialist forces in the sub-region experience serious difficulties in the struggle for social transformations and peace not only because they have to counter the policy of the reformist and pro-imperialist parties but also because the trade union movement is basically at the service of the US monopolies. As in Great Britain, the Caribbean trade unions are traditionally linked with the main political groups. As such, they played a positive role in the 30's and 40's. With the advent of the Cold War, however, their leadership departed from a progressive course, linking with the opportunist International Confederation of Free Trade Unions. Through labour colleges and institutes funded by US capital, the CIA inculcates anti-communism and renunciation of the class struggle in trade unionists. For this reason, the trade union movement either plays an openly counter-revolutionary role, as it did in Guyana in 1962-1964, or co-operates with capital, betraying the interests of the workers.

Control of the media by the local bourgeoisie, linked with Anglo-US imperialism, creates additional difficulties in the masses' struggle for national liberation and peace. A January 1984 conference of cultural and intellectual workers in defence of the sovereignty of the sub-region's countries drew attention to this fact. It condemned the US invasion of Grenada and noted that "in the coverage of the invasion sections of the Caribbean media demonstrated a shameless and obsequious willingness to serve as the apologists of the invaders of Caribbean sovereignty... that in a region with some twenty-seven radio stations, at least twelve of them directly or indirectly state-owned, and some twelve television stations, all but one state-owned, we are subjected to a diet of vulgar foreign programming in which Caribbean people see themselves negated..." The conference recognized the need to place the mass media at the service of the peoples.

The sharp ideological and political struggle around the roads of development in the Caribbean sub-region therefore continues. Its prospects are going to depend to a decisive extent on how deeply instilled in the masses' consciousness is the necessity to strengthen peace and end the arms race.

FACTORS FAVOURING PEACE

The growing isolation of the United States in international organizations, the increasing opposition to Reagan's militarist policy and the contradictions in the camp of imperialism aid the development of the peace movement.

The United States was criticized at the UN Special Session on Disarmament for failure to adopt a reasonable disarmament programme. Praising the Soviet Union for making new proposals and "assuming an unequivocal obligation not to be the first to use nuclear weapons", UN Secretary General Javier Perez de Cuellar declared that "if all states that have nuclear weapons were to make such a pledge and were to adhere to it, this would be tantamount in practice to banning the use of nuclear weapons altogether."

The socialist states, loyal allies of the peoples championing their national independence and sovereignty, categorically condemned the US aggression against Grenada and are giving full support to Nicaragua and the liberation movements in the Caribbean. They are contributing greatly towards making our sub-region a zone of peace.

Inside the United States, a growing body of public opinion favours disarmament and peace. *Time* magazine conducted a poll which showed that 93 per cent of Americans support thinking in terms of peaceful solutions.[14] The US Congress, and even the Republican-controlled Senate, are showing increasing opposition to Reagan's adventurist policies in Central America. Washington's refusal to abide by the decisions of the International Court in the Hague on terrorist activity against the people and government of Nicaragua[15] exposes the United States as a violator of the rule of law and as a country practising state terrorism.

The invasion of Grenada evoked strong criticisms from many member states of the international community, including America's NATO allies. At an OAS session, several delegates openly called Washington's Grenadian adventures "a flagrant and brutal violation of the principle of non-intervention and the OAS Charter". Representatives of thirteen of the eighteen states participating in the session warned that the invasion violated the principles of self-determination and respect for the territorial integrity of one of the members of the Latin American regional organization. Condemning the United States invasion of Grenada, Luis Echeverria, former President of Mexico and Vice-President of the World Peace Council, pointed out that it was one more act that endangers world peace and must be related to the arms race and the preparations for a nuclear war.

Opinion is also shifting in a favourable direction in Great Britain. In a report published in December 1982, the Foreign

Affairs Committee of the British House of Commons was critical of US policy in our sub-region, noting that "a view of the Caribbean Basin dominated by the belief that it is a theatre of East-West confrontation provides an unsatisfactory and insufficient policy framework", placing too much emphasis on the containment of communism and too little on the need to help regional states "solve their own problems in their own way".[16]

The French government agreed to help in sweeping the mines to the approaches of Nicaragua's ports. Earlier, in 1981, the French and Mexican governments recognized the Farabundo Marti Liberation Front and the Revolutionary Democratic Front of El Salvador as a "representative political force"; they also called for a negotiated political settlement in that country. The Contadora group is playing a positive role in the effort to find a peaceful solution to the problems of Central America and the Caribbean.

The victory of the democratic and progressive forces in Argentina, the heroic resistance of the Chilean people, the struggles of the working people of the Dominican Republic and other countries against IMF diktat, and the mass upsurge of Brazilians for direct presidential elections positively influence the Caribbean peace movement.

The Non-Aligned Movement is also a great force in the anti-war struggle. The Havana and New Delhi summits of 1979 and 1983 placed on the US the prime responsibility for the arms race and many social evils facing the underdeveloped countries.

The servile role played by some Caribbean countries in the invasion of Grenada cannot obscure the underlying contradictions between the region and the United States. The heads of almost all countries of the sub-region have condemned the paltry sum offered by Reagan's Caribbean Basin Initiative and protested against the aid terms, which openly endanger sovereignty. Washington's military backing of the fascist regime in Guatemala also alienates the CARICOM countries, which support Belize in its struggle against the Guatemalan dictatorship to maintain its territorial integrity.

Thus we have an aggregate of factors which indicates a growing rebuff to the aggressive US course in the Caribbean.

THE COMMUNIST POSITION

In the aggravated regional and international situation, the Communists of the Caribbean have a big role to play in promoting peace. In order to win over the masses from the influence of petty-bourgeois and social-democratic ideology, they must struggle against rightist and leftist opportunism, anti-communism and its special brand - anti-Sovietism. And, of course, the fraternal parties must actively fight for detente for it was under conditions of detente that positive gains were made in the Caribbean in the 1975-1980 period. We believe that the Latin American Economic System (SELA)[17] should be strengthened as an independent regional organization.

The Communists are forging anti-imperialist unity in each territory and creating revolutionary-democratic unity on a regional scale to counter the divide-and-rule policy of imperialism. They are combating both "geographical fatalism"[18] and Caribbean "exceptionalism".[19] The Communists of the Caribbean are making their contribution to the unity of the three revolutionary streams - the world system of socialism, the national liberation movement and the working class of the capitalist world. The Communist parties and left-wing groups must be strengthened organizationally and be capable of creatively applying in practice the theoretical principles of Marxism-Leninism. We are also seeking to step up party work in the trade unions. This is absolutely necessary to remove the influence of opportunism on them.

National independence and advance towards socialism have been on the agenda for many years in the Commonwealth Caribbean. In this sense, the two phases of the revolution -

national liberation and social emancipation - are interlinked. There is a merging of the struggle against imperialism and against local reaction. However, since imperialism is the main prop of the big landlord, monopoly and financial oligarchy and is mainly responsible for dependency, backwardness, dictatorship and fascism, it is necessary to project a democratic, anti-imperialist alternative at the first stage.

At the same time, in countries such as Barbados and Trinidad and Tobago where long-established right-wing social-democratic parties operate, it is very important not only to formulate such an alternative but also to show the prospects opened up by scientific socialism. As Lenin pointed out, the role of vanguard fighter can be fulfilled only by a party that is guided by the most advanced theory.

In carrying out their national and international tasks, the Marxist-Leninist parties in the sub-region must exercise extreme care and flexibility. They have to work out an alliance policy with social circles either inside or/and outside the government. The Communists must take anti-imperialist action in common with the ruling groups while at the same time, in close co-operation with other democratic and subversive forces, vigorously oppose the governments' anti-labour and anti-people actions. We believe that if unlimited, uncritical support is given to their anti-imperialist positions without struggle in defence of the working people's rights, the results can be catastrophic for the Communists organisationally and numerically, especially where the ruling political forces restrict in every possible way the activity of the revolutionary vanguard, which holds to the positions of scientific socialism. In Guyana, for example, socialism is being discredited. Imperialist propaganda and local reaction claim that this country has demonstrated that "socialism" means no bread, no basic necessities, flight from starvation (emigration), rigged elections and denial of human rights.

A consultative meeting of Caribbean Communist and revolutionary-democratic parties and organizations convened on the PPP's initiative in March 1984 in Guyana focused on the problems created by the Grenada events and set tasks to counter the imperialist offensive, safeguard peace, ensure the sovereignty, independence and territorial integrity of all Caribbean states, and improve the people's well-being. The meeting was unanimous that the deteriorating economic situation and the declining living standards in our zone endanger peace and security. The Reagan-sponsored CBI was assessed as an instrument aimed at creating a military-political bloc serving imperialism and directed against the people's interests. The final document stressed the need to counter the USA's aggressive course, and denounced the growing militarisation of the Caribbean and in particular the Washington-supported and controlled Eastern Caribbean interventionist army.

The consultative meeting noted the increasing dangers facing the Nicaraguan revolution and expressed its wholehearted support and solidarity with the people and government of Nicaragua, the revolutionary forces of El Salvador and fraternal Cuba, which is successfully building a socialist society. The meeting also underscored the need to step up the fight for world peace and to make the Caribbean a zone of peace.

These questions were discussed at the first consultative meeting of anti-imperialist organizations of Central America and the Caribbean held in June 1984 in Havana and attended by representatives of over thirty parties and national liberation movements. The joint communiqué reflected a uniform assessment of the explosive situation brought about in the region by Washington, and noted that both the victims of the armed adventures and the region's other countries affected by the crisis of the world capitalist economy, mass unemployment, hunger and poverty, are feeling imperialism's pressure.

The strategy and tactics of the struggle against US expansion and the tyranny of its puppets were collectively worked out, the immediate goal being co-ordinated actions in support of socialist Cuba, all possible assistance to revolutionary Nicaragua, the development of solidarity with the patriots of El Salvador, Guatemala and other countries, and a broad campaign in defence of the people of occupied Grenada. Long-term objectives were also formulated: liquidation of the foreign military bases and prevention of nuclear weapons deployment in the sub-region; prohibition of military, economic and political aggression in any form; non-use of mercenaries; elimination of some countries' colonial dependence on imperialist monopolies; strict observance of the principle of non-interference in the internal affairs of states; an end to manoeuvres and the disbanding of the military blocs knocked together in the region by Washington.

A meeting of Communist parties of South America (July 1984, Buenos Aires) also opposed the United States' imperialist pressure on the peoples of Central America and the Caribbean and denounced Washington's criminal actions. The meeting also discussed burning problems such as US intervention in Central America, the ploys against the Nicaraguan revolution and the threat to the continent's democratic governments on the part of the reactionary military cliques. Pointing to the growth in US imperialism's aggressiveness in the international arena, the meeting stressed that in Latin America it took its crudest form in relations with socialist Cuba and revolutionary Nicaragua.

Trade and economic relations between the USA and the underdeveloped states were not equitable, the final communiqué noted. Regularly causing interest rates to rise, Washington used the Latin American countries' difficult economic situation, notably the foreign debt repayment problem, as an instrument of diktat and enslavement. The White House was bent on forcing the peoples of the continent to pay for the arms race, which the United States had been intensifying.

The document emphasised that the Reagan Administration was pursuing a militarist policy in an effort to expose humanity to the risk of a nuclear catastrophe. This policy contrasted sharply with the Soviet Union's peace initiatives and ran counter to the demands of all people of goodwill.

The special feature of the present period is that preparations are under way for direct aggression against Nicaragua which will mean intervention against all of Central America and the Caribbean to suppress the movement for national liberation and social emancipation. Once it has started here, the United States could plunge the entire world into the nightmare of a total nuclear war. The Communists and all progressive forces of the Caribbean call on the peoples to repel this policy vigorously

July 1984

[1] *Newsweek*, May 1984.

[2] CARIFTA, set up in 1968 under an agreement signed in St John's (Antigua), united both independent states and British possessions, and the so-called associated countries under Britain's control. CARIFTA included Barbados, Guyana, Antigua, Trinidad and Tobago, Jamaica, Belize, Grenada, Dominica, Montserrat, St Vincent, St Lucia and St Christopher-Nevis-Anguilla. Its founders saw it as the first stage towards the Caribbean Common Market (CCM), which was established in 1973.

[3] Hillbourne Watson, 'United States Policy Towards the Caribbean,' presented to CEESTEM Conference, March 1982, Mexico, p. 128.

[4] CARICOM, a political and economic association of Caribbean countries formed in 1973 on the basis of CARIFTA.

[5] A regional economic development bank set up in 1979 to serve CARICOM and the CCM.

[6] One in which the bauxite is not sent for processing but is merely stored.

[7] In Guyana debt and compensation payments increased from 15% of current revenue in 1964 to 92% in 1983; while debt servicing absorbed 10% of foreign currency earnings in 1977, that figure increased to 42% in 1983.

[8] Ex-Prime Minister, virtual dictator of Grenada. Over-thrown by the 1979 revolution, he fled to the USA, returning to the island in 1983 following the invasion by US troops.

[9] A development model forcibly imposed on Puerto Rico by Washington. Its essence is complete political and economic dependence on the US.

[10] Reagan made this initiative in February 1982, promising the Caribbean and Central America about $350 million as "aid" (in the 1982 fiscal year) and guaranteed US markets for their traditional exports. It was proposed that in response these countries should create favourable conditions for US monopolies on their territories and fully support Washington's policy. For more details see: Cheddi Jagan, 'The Caribbean Danger Zone,' *World Marxist Review*, No. 8, 1983.

[11] 'Vere Bird's Defence Force Warning', *Caribbean Contact*, Barbados, April 1983, p. 13.

[12] Prior to 1983 the US had only one Ambassador (resident in Grenada) to all the Eastern Caribbean countries.

[13] This concept, taken from bourgeois politology, signifies active state participation in society's economic life.

[14] *Time*, January 2, 1984, p.2.

[15] This refers to the May 1984 decision of the International Court, which unanimously obliged the US immediately to end any action impeding entry into or exit from Nicaraguan ports and to refrain from such actions in future. The court also decided that Nicaragua's right to sovereignty and political independence must be respected and must not be endangered by any military or paramilitary operations prohibited by international law.

[16] Jeremy Taylor, 'Rediscovering the Caribbean,' *The Caribbean Chronicle*, West India Committee, February/March 1983, p. 10.

[17] SELA, set up 1975, is the economic community of Latin American countries. It includes almost thirty states of South America, Central America and the Caribbean. The formation of SELA with Cuba's participation and without the US is a reflection of the community's determination to achieve economic independence and end the domination of the transnational companies.

[18] A concept which says that there can be no revolution in Latin American countries because of the subregion's proximity to the USA.

[19] A sectarian position rejecting the application of the general propositions of Marxist-Leninist theory to the Caribbean.

CHAPTER FOUR

THEORY OF VITAL INTERESTS AND SECURITY ZONES[1]

"Under what international law do we have a right to attempt to destabilize a constitutionally-elected Government of another country?" That was how the question was put by a journalist to President Ford after the Popular Unity Government of Salvador Allende was overthrown with the complicity of the CIA[2] The President replied: "I am not going to pass judgement on whether it is permitted or authorised under international law. It is a recognized fact that historically as well as presently such actions are taken in the best interest of the countries involved".

President Ford arrogated to himself the right to determine not only what was best for his country but for another sovereign independent country, Chile. Under Presidents James Carter and Ronald Reagan, "best interests" became "vital interests".

All states have vital interests. In general these are the welfare and security of their citizens; as the American Declaration of Independence broadly put it: life, liberty and the pursuit of happiness. As such, the nation-state has security interests - protection of sovereignty, national independence and territorial integrity.

Socio-economically, however, states are different and different kinds of states serve different national, class and social ends, and use different means, even intervention and war, sometimes in contravention of the rule of law, to justify ends.

The socio-economic system of capitalism, based on the private ownership of the means of production, distribution and exchange and the exploitation of man by man, developed from the early competitive stage to the present state-monopoly stage. In the course of its historical development, the law of unequal development led to inter-state and inter-imperialist rivalry and wars for territorial gains as sources of raw materials and markets for goods and capital.

At the metropole in the developed capitalist states, the class struggle sharpened leading in the case of Russia to the October Socialist Revolution in 1917. The first workers' state, the Soviet Union, set as its goal the socialisation of the means of production and the end of the exploitative system. Its first foreign policy document was the Decree on Peace. It proclaimed "the key principles of Soviet foreign policy: the struggle for peace and peaceful coexistence between states with different social and economic systems, proletarian internationalism, recognition of complete equality of all peoples, respect for sovereignty and independence and finally, non-interference in their internal affairs".[3] It proposed that relations between states with different socio-economic systems must be based not on militarism and war, but on peaceful competition. The West was not prepared to co-operate with the Soviet Union on the basis of peaceful coexistence, normalisation of inter-state relations, and economic co-operation. Instead, in 1918-20, perceiving in the new socio-economic system of socialism/communism a threat to their vital, but in fact class, interest, 14 capitalist states intervened in the Soviet Union to destroy the first workers' state, the declared aim being, as Winston Churchill graphically described it, to strangle the communist "infant in its cradle".

The Bolsheviks were treated like international outcasts. In the 1930's, the West refused to work out a system of collective security advocated by the USSR and to take collective action to block military aggression by fascist Germany and Italy on

Republican Spain and Abyssinia (Ethiopia) respectively, a refusal which led to World War II. The USSR, having failed to achieve security through collective action, resorted at first to a bilateral treaty (USSR - Germany) to protect her national interests. When this Treaty was breached, and under Hitlerite fascism (decadent, terroristic state-monopoly capitalism) another attempt was made in the interest of "peace and security" to liquidate the Soviet State, the Soviet people in co-operation with others fought heroically to defend their homeland and to defeat world fascism.

Meanwhile, at the periphery, under dependent/distorted capitalism, the struggle for national and social liberation intensified. The peoples in the colonial and dependent territories also wanted independence, freedom and democracy, which were enunciated in the Atlantic Charter of 1941. This struggle eventually led to the liquidation of the system of colonialism, and the establishment of many revolutionary democratic, socialist-oriented and socialist states.

The resultant shift in the world balance of forces in favour of socialism was/is perceived by world capitalism/imperialism as a threat to 'vital interest'. To counter that threat, an obsessive mentality developed and myths were created, leading to the establishment of 'national security' states and security zones for the maintenance of the status quo. Militarisation, repression and intervention are justified in the name of security and sovereignty, while human-centred values such as truth, social justice, freedom and human solidarity are undercut and sacrificed at home and overseas.

THE USA AND VITAL INTEREST

The United States of America has a long history of reliance on military force and wars, mostly unjust, to secure its 'vital interests'. It developed into the foremost capitalist/imperialist state through various phases: a war of national liberation to attain independence; wars to expand its national boundary; a civil war to establish the hegemony of the bourgeoisie over the slave-owning oligarchy; external expansion, particularly in Latin America, by a militaristic ('big stick') policy; a co-operative/competitive relationship with other capitalist states - co-operative in the fight against socialism/communism, and competitive to gain hegemony in the world capitalist system.

On a foundation of slavery and capitalist dependency, the Americans in the 13 North American British colonies waged, with French material assistance - arms and men including the famous General Lafayette - a just war of national liberation. The Declaration of Independence of 1776 was a populist -democratic document, but the Constitution which emerged 11years later established the supremacy of the propertied classes and interests.

The ideology and rationale for national territorial expansion and influence abroad was provided by various declarations and acts in the interest of the slave-owning homesteads and the bourgeois nationalists.

The doctrine of Manifest Destiny[4] of 1819 laid the basis for the seizure of lands from the American Indians and Mexicans - "the lesser breeds without the Law".

The Monroe Doctrine[5] of 1823 couched US expansionist tendency in democratic phraseology. With the 'non-colonization' principle, the United States warned the European powers to observe a 'hands-off', 'non-interference' policy towards the Western hemisphere and staked out its own claim to the region. In his message to Congress in 1823, President Monroe said: "We should consider any attempt on their part to extend their system to any portion of this hemisphere as dangerous to our peace and safety".

The Civil War in 1864 between the capitalist North over the slave-holding South placed power in the hands of the big bourgeoisie. In their interest, America fought a war with Spain in 1898 to carve out its own colonial empire in the 20th century, 'the American Century'.

The Roosevelt Corollary[6] of 1904 justified 'big stick' intervention in the domestic affairs of 'unstable' countries on the grounds that instability was a threat to 'civilization'. The Wilson Doctrine, [7] based on a free enterprise philosophy and 'Open Door' policy, created the conditions overseas for US goods and investments.

President Woodrow Wilson encouraged US involvement in a struggle to "command the economic fortunes of the world". Intervention in the USSR and elsewhere was justified on the ground of unfitness. Wilson set about to "teach the South American republics to elect good men" and to establish a government in Mexico "under which all contracts and business and concessions will be safer than they have been". And if governments persisted in being non-conformist and revolutionary, then the weapon of non-recognition was utilised.

In the era of 'dollar diplomacy', defined by President Taft as a "policy... characterised as substituting dollars for bullets", foreign investment was given protection. On April 25, 1927, President Coolidge pointed out that, although the USA would not think of interfering "in the purely domestic affairs" of other states, "there was a distinct and binding obligation on the part of self-respecting governments to afford protection to the persons and property of their citizens, wherever they may be".[8]

THE COLD WAR

The spokesmen of capitalism/imperialism, President Harry Truman and Winston Churchill, seeing their world shrinking, at the end of World War II embarked on an ideological crusade against socialism/communism. Narrow self-interest was clothed in emotional phrase-mongering like "Western spiritual values" and "Christian civilization". But President Truman laid bare the real motivation when he pointed out that governments which conducted planned economies and controlled foreign trade were dangers to freedom, that freedom of speech and worship were dependent on the free enterprise system. He pointed out that controlled economies were "not the American way" and "not the way of peace". He urged that "the whole world should adopt the American system" and "the American system could survive in America only if it became a World System". Calling for action, he implored: "Unless we act and act decisively, it [government-controlled economy and government-controlled foreign trade] will be the pattern of the next century ... if this trend is not reversed, the government of the United States will be under pressure, sooner or later, to use these same devices to fight for markets and for raw materials".[9]

With the Truman Doctrine of 1947, the Cold War was launched, a rabid anti-socialist and anti-national liberation campaign under the doctrine of the "containment of communism". While the immediate objective of world capitalism/imperialism was the shoring-up of counter-revolution and reaction in Greece and Turkey, the strategic aim was a halt to radicalism and revolution in general and to socialism/communism in particular.

Containment was to be global in view of the perceived 'Soviet threat'. NSC-68 (The Report of the Secretaries of State and Defence on United States Objectives and Progress for National Security, April 7, 1950,) claimed that the Soviet Union wanted to impose its absolute authority over the rest of the world; that any failure to defend a position would demoralise US allies, and eventually "by gradual withdrawals under pressure ... we (shall) discover one day that we have sacrificed 'vital interest'".[10]

Truman's "containment of communism" included a comprehensive military, political, economic and 'psychological warfare' programme. These were: the bypassing of the United Nations 'collective security' approach; the creation of the Central Intelligence Agency (CIA) through the National Security Act (1947) and the Central Intelligence Agency Act (1949) for intelligence gathering and covert actions; the establishment of 'national security' states; the promulgation of the Inter-American Treaty for Reciprocal Assistance (Rio Pact) for the military unification of Latin America and the Caribbean under the aegis of the Pentagon; the establishment of the Organization of American States (OAS) for the political/legal subjugation of the Western Hemisphere; the launching of 'Point Four' and 'Marshall

Plan' aid-programmes as an integral part of the US military mobilisation; the establishment of military bases world-wide for the encirclement of the USSR and other socialist states.

Spearheaded against the national liberation movements, the Rio Pact established a 'security zone' area which was three times larger than the 'neutral zone' area established at a conference in Panama in September 1939. Its establishment was a violation of the norms of international law on freedom of navigation and of territorial waters.[11] Bilateral military treaties were also signed with several Latin American and Caribbean States reducing them virtually to client-states[12] of the USA. Military aid was stepped up for the oligarchy. In return, the US obtained military bases.

The Rio Pact and the OAS formed the basis of a world-wide network of politico-military security zones. These included:

> 1) The North Atlantic Treaty of April 1949, associating the United States and Western Europe, together with Greece and Turkey; and the Organization of European Economic Co-operation (Marshall Plan authority);
>
> 2) The Bonn and Paris Treaties for including a remilitarised Western Germany in the Western military bloc;
>
> 3) The Balkan Pact of Turkey, Greece and Yugoslavia;
>
> 4) The Middle Eastern series of military pacts, including the United States treaties with Turkey and Pakistan, the Turkey-Pakistan Treaty, and the Baghdad Treaty of Britain, Iraq, Pakistan, Turkey and Iran in February 1954 (replaced by CENTO after the Iraq revolution of 1958);
>
> 5) The South East Asia Treaty of September 8, 1954 of the five imperialist powers interested in the region, together with Pakistan, Thailand and the Philippines (after the communist victory in China in 1949, the US fiasco in

Korea in 1950-51, and the disastrous French defeat at Dien Bien Phu in Vietnam in 1954);

6) The Pacific Pact of the United States, Australia and New Zealand (ANZUS) in 1951;

7) The Far Eastern Treaties of the United States with Japan, Chiang Kai-shek and Syngman Rhee.

The 'Cold War' shattered the anti-Hitlerite coalition and launched a crusade against "communism from within and without". Inside the United States, anti-Red hysteria, neo-fascist McCarthyism[13] and a 'national security' psychosis were instituted under the Smith Act (June 1940), the Voorhis Act (October 1940), the McCarran Act (1950) and the Communist Control Act (1954) to fight the alleged internal enemy, the communists, who were deemed 'agents of Moscow' and international communism. The Communist Party of the USA was deemed a 'subversive' organization, and many communists and progressives were witch-hunted, persecuted and jailed. With the connivance of Washington, 'national security' states were established in various regions of the world.

Nuclear blackmail was resorted to. Preparations went ahead for the encirclement of, and a possible pre-emptive nuclear strike against, the Soviet Union. Reliance was placed on force to safeguard 'vital interest'. Imperialist aggression took many forms: direct military intervention (against the PPP government in British Guiana in 1953 and later in the Dominican Republic in 1965, Vietnam, Grenada in 1983, etc); indirect military intervention (Guatemala in 1954, Cuba in 1961, etc); CIA destabilisation (Iran in 1953, British Guiana against the third PPP government in 1962-64, Chile in 1973, Jamaica in 1976 and 1980, etc); economic blockade and sabotage; and psychological warfare.

Statistics put out by the Brookings Institution (USA) point out: "... from 1946 to 1975, the USA had recourse to direct and indirect armed force in 215 instances." James West, Political Bureau member of the Communist Party of the USA, noted:

> In Washington's top echelons the possibility of using nuclear weapons was discussed nineteen times, and four times directly against the Soviet Union. All in all, since 1945 the USA initiated or participated in most military conflicts, in which over ten million people died.[14]

President Dwight Eisenhower, an exponent of military policy based on 'peace through strength' and a 'massive retaliation strategy,' shifted the militarisation programme from 'containment' to 'liberation' and 'roll back'. Perturbed by developments in the Middle East in the 1950's - the overthrow of the Shah of Iran and King Farouk of Egypt; the nationalization of the Anglo-Iranian Oil Company; the Egypt-Czechoslovakia trade deal (cotton in exchange for factories and arms); the nationalization of the Suez Canal Company; the Anglo-French-Israeli fiasco in Egypt in 1956 - the United States, under the Eisenhower Doctrine, declared that it would intervene in the Middle East to prevent political instability and the spread of international communism which might endanger its vital interests, particularly oil.[15]

President John F Kennedy vowed to get "America moving again". His special brand of containment was 'limited response', instead of the 'brinkmanship' of President Dwight Eisenhower and Secretary of State John Foster Dulles, and a flexible 'club and carrot' policy; that is counter-insurgency and reformism — counter-insurgency with Green Berets and the CIA to ensure that there would be "no more Cubas" and reformism to ensure that there would be evolution, not revolution. To counter the example and attraction of the Cuban revolution, the Alliance for Progress was launched in 1961 as a reformist aid programme. It was conditional on agrarian, taxation, financial, administrative and other reforms; private sector development; and an annual economic growth rate of 2.5 per cent. It failed to attain its objectives and finally collapsed.

On the excuse of saving American lives and preventing a communist take-over, President Johnson intervened in 1965 with a massive military invasion in the Dominican Republic. With the Johnson Doctrine,[16] the US assumed the right to intervene in any country of the Americas where communists were likely to take power, and greatly expanded the scope of direct US military intervention in the "dirty war"[17] against Vietnam.

With the attainment of strategic equality or parity in the late 1960's and early 1970's between the USA and USSR, and a change in the balance of forces between the world's two opposing socio-economic systems, US policy shifted to new methods of containment, to the doctrine of 'realistic deterrence'. A dual outlook developed towards the socialist community by the ruling circles: the realistic elements in the United States and some West European countries moving towards peaceful co-existence; and the 'war party' linked to the military-industrial complex wanting to continue confrontation with the socialist countries and the national liberation forces. As regards the latter, the Nixon Doctrine, recognizing that the United States could no longer alone sustain the cost of 'world policeman', declared that that role must be shared by other states in different regions. President Nixon's 'Vietnamisation' policy against the national liberation movement was based on 'Third World' peoples providing the lives, the USA providing the dollars and certain autocratic client-states playing the role of regional 'policemen'.

NON-ALIGNMENT AND PEACEFUL CO-EXISTENCE

Perceiving the offensive military treaties and bases in pursuit of the policy of 'containment' and 'roll-back' as a threat to their vital interests, and faced with the rearmament of West Germany and its inclusion in the Western military bloc, the Soviet Union and the People's Democracies of East Europe established in 1955 the defensive military Warsaw Pact.

Many developing countries did not see their interests served by being a member of either the imperialist or the socialist military bloc, and moved to a Non-Aligned position.

However, for national and historical reasons, the Non-Aligned states had more in common with the Socialist Community than with the Western Alliance. They had suffered at the hands of imperialism and from the pangs of colonialism and neo-colonialism, and many embraced some form of socialism. On many vital issues, the positions of the Non-Aligned Movement and the socialist states coincided. The coincidence of views on important questions led to the successful outcome of the Afro-Asian Conference held at Bandung, Indonesia in April 1955.

Non-Alignment was welcomed by the Soviet Union and attacked by the USA. The 20th Congress of the Communist Party of the Soviet Union welcomed the Bandung Conference as representing "the best formula of relations between countries with different social systems under present circumstances and would serve as the basis for stable peaceful relations between all countries of the world". US Secretary of State John Foster Dulles described Non-Alignment as an "obsolete" and "immoral and short-sighted conception".[18]

Presidents John F Kennedy, Lyndon Johnson and James Carter manoeuvred to shift the Non-Aligned Movement from its fundamental principles against colonialism, neo-colonialism, imperialism, Zionism, apartheid and all forms of racial discrimination, and peaceful co-existence to a US-style of neutralism, democratic in form, but pro-imperialist in content.

President Lyndon Johnson called for the creation of one big "ideological family", the replacement of "geographical frontiers" by "ideological frontiers" for the preservation of freedom and democracy, a euphemism for capitalism/imperialism. He proposed the grouping of Third World and Non-Aligned countries into regional alliances (Free Trade Areas and Common Markets) under the control of imperialism and the transnational monopolies.[19]

To influence the course of socio-political transformations and to shape "a rapidly changing world in ways that would be congenial to our interests and responsive to our values" Carter's Security Adviser Zbigniew Brezezinski urged not a regional but a differentiated country to country approach "where they demonstrate independence from Moscow and willingness to contribute to overall regional stability, we should encourage them. Where they do not, we should isolate them."

The Santa Fe Committee's ideologues of the Reagan administration accused the Carter administration of being too soft with the socialist world, working for an "anxious accommodation" as "if we would prevent the political coloration of Latin America to red crimson by an American-prescribed tint of pale pink, giving encouragement to socialism and change in the Non-Aligned countries and of alienating traditional 'friends' with its human rights fervour, thus sacrificing US 'vital interests'."

DETENTE AND PEACE

The United States entered the 1970's with a serious economic crisis lasting for two years until 1972. Another crisis in 1974-75, the sixth in the post-war period was more far-reaching than the 1929-1933 depression. World capitalism was faced with recession and 'stagflation'. And the huge Vietnam war expenditure of nearly $60 billion (US) annually in the closing years also seriously affected the US economy - balance of trade and balance of payments deficits; non-convertibility of the US dollar; devaluations in 1971 and 1973.

At the same time the undeclared, unpopular Vietnam war rocked the United States to its foundations. There was a groundswell of discontent among the masses, particularly students, intellectuals and working people, black and white. For the American people, this biggest imperialist debacle in the post-World War II period was costly both in lives and welfare.

In this changed situation, a new attitude of introspection, if not isolation, developed in the United States. Everything was seriously questioned. The 'war on want' was an abysmal failure. Militarism and the US role as 'world policeman' was distrusted. Rich as it was, it could not afford at one and the same time a guns-and-butter policy. The new mood, downplaying the military aspect, emphasised peaceful means and search for new ways to maintain US hegemony.

The three groups of the US capitalist ruling class pressed for policies favourable to their own, and at times conflicting, interests. The 'dirty war' in Vietnam had proved to be bad for business, except for the big corporations linked with the Pentagon, the arms industry and the military-industrial complex which constituted the first of the three groups within US capitalist ruling circles. The second group, the transnational corporations engaged in investment and trade overseas, was faced with a generally hostile anti-American attitude worldwide. It also met with increasing competition from Japan and the EEC, and growing assertiveness by the 'Third World', particularly Non-Aligned, countries for more equitable economic relations and national recuperation of natural resources under a New International Economic Order (NIEO).

With the threat of nationalization, and particularly the Arab oil boycott of 1973, the transnational corporations of USA, Western Europe and Japan constituted the Trilateral Commission, and mooted the idea of "equal partnership" and "global interdependence"; they fought for a "favourable investment climate" in the developing countries and moved to establish "joint enterprises" under their control [20] They wanted the abandonment of the old hard-line militarist tradition, and a less aggressive and more subtle foreign policy - a move from confrontation and military intervention to co-operation and collusion. Detente became a political imperative.

The third group of the US capitalist ruling class, engaged mainly in civilian production for the domestic market, was hard hit by stagflation. Increases in the price of fuel (oil) added to their woes. For this, they blamed the big oil monopolies, the 'seven sisters'. Noting that recession was leading not only to lower turnover and profits, but also to ruin and bankruptcy, they saw in the normalisation of East-West trading relations the possibility for the expansion of the domestic market. Thus, they too favoured detente.

Consequently, the strengthened pacifist wing of American ruling circles opted for peaceful co-existence.

An atmosphere of tranquility was developed in international relations; Cold War gave way to an alternative - detente. Dr Henry Kissinger embarked on a programme of 'shuttle diplomacy', and President Nixon visited China, Poland and the Soviet Union for the purpose of bridge-building.

NUCLEAR MADNESS

The Arab oil boycott of 1973, the fall of the Shah in 1979 and the loss of Iran as the second largest Middle East oil exporter and one of the most important imperialist forward military outposts, together with revolutions in Ethiopia, Afghanistan, Nicaragua, Grenada and elsewhere caused consternation in US ruling circles. National Security Adviser, Zbigniew Brezezinski, described the area from Pakistan to Ethiopia and the Middle East including the Persian Gulf and the Red Sea as the "arc of crisis" or "arc of instability". He pinpointed United States dependence of foreign countries for 26 of the 31 basic raw materials,[21] including oil, consumed by US industry. The Caribbean was described as the "fourth trouble spot".

President James Carter, on assuming office had declared that the United States was no longer driven by the "inordinate fear of communism" and had embraced ideological pluralism and human rights doctrine; later he placed "an emphasis on the external threat to the West posed by the Soviet Union". His administration reactivated the Cold War, embarked on an expanded militarisation programme for the purpose of "protecting American interests and ensuring the uninterrupted flow of Arab oil". This five-year programme provided for real military expenditures averaging over 4.5% a year and including the updating of the country's arms arsenal - the new MX mobile intercontinental ballistic missile, the Trident ballistic missile - firing submarine, cruise missiles, modernised B-52 bombers, etc - and the strengthening of the 'rapid deployment forces.' Prior to the late 1960's, US policy relied mainly on 'forward basing' - large concentraion of US troops overseas. But as a result of heavy cost and objections from progressive forces, the concept of 'strategic mobility' was embraced and emphasis was shifted to 'rapid deployment forces' and to the production of highly sophisticated, particularly nuclear, weaponry.

A military so-called peace-keeping force was mooted for Latin America and the Caribbean. President Carter's Directive 52 detailed actions to check Cuba's influence in the Caribbean and her military support for Third World countries. It also called for the transfer to the Caribbean Contingency Joint Task Force, if necessary, of "airborne troops, naval strike units, the Marines, or whatever forces are deemed necessary by him and the Joint Chiefs of Staff to contain the Caribbean".[22]

With the Carter Doctrine, the United States committed itself to the military intervention in the Persian Gulf region, which was deemed "of vital security interest". Before the invasion of Grenada, Dr Richard Feinburg, a State Department Specialist on Latin American affairs, declared in Barbados that if US vital interests were threatened, the use of military force would become an option. An agreement was reached with the Dominican Republic for co-operation in fighting the 'communist threat', and for the Dominican armed forces to aid the Duvalier dictatorship should it come under attack. And Presidential Directive PD-59, which substituted a 'counterforce' nuclear war-fighting policy for the 'deterrence' policy, mooted the idea of a 'limited' nuclear war, deemed by the world press as "nuclear madness directives".

The excuse for the military escalation was the bogey of a 'Soviet military threat'. For its assistance to Democratic Afghanistan, the Soviet Union was charged with "violating international law", and posing a "threat to world security". This charge was patently false. Actually, long before Soviet assistance was rendered in December 1979, and precisely a month after the Saur revolution in April 1978, the NATO Council meeting in Washington had agreed to increase military budgets of all member-states by 3% per year until the end of the century. And in December 1979, the Brussels session of the NATO Council under US pressure took a decision on the production and deployment of 572 Tomahawk cruise missiles and Pershing-2 ballistic missiles in several West European countries.

Three main factors contributed to a move away from detente and a policy of parity and equal security and towards a 'guns-before-butter', 'military superiority' and 'first-strike capability' policy. Firstly, the military-industrial-complex had failed to turn detente to their advantage; secondly, the outlook of the three sections of the US capitalist ruling class had converged in relation to US foreign policy after the Iranian revolution. The section of the US bourgeoisie concerned with military production lost about $14 billion through cancellation of huge military contracts; the transnational corporations suffered from the seizure of about $8 billion of property, and the group producing for the domestic market saw the cut-off of Iranian oil and the consequent shortages and increased prices as inimical to their interests. Thirdly, the popularity of President Carter, who had been elected with a mandate of only 28% of the adult population in 1976 when 54.4% of the electorate had voted, had declined quite sharply. With the economic situation out of control, it became imperative to concentrate attention on military and foreign policy problems long before the elections, and to pursue a course of aggravating international tensions on the ground that the Soviet Union was posing a danger to the 'national security' of the USA.

Familiar Cold War moves, some contrary to international law, were again undertaken. The US Ambassador was recalled from Moscow; the Soviet Union was forced to reduce its diplomatic staff in the USA; a 17 million ton sale of wheat was stopped; SALT II was withdrawn from the Senate floor; computer and other technology sales were shelved; and the Moscow Olympics was boycotted. The US-China axis was to be strengthened. Pakistan, with a bloody dictator seeking to manufacture the nuclear bomb, would be armed to the teeth. And the reactionary feudal elements of Afghanistan would be fully supported.

The Reagan administration's policies were blueprinted by the ultra-conservative Committee of Santa Fe in its report 'A New Inter-American Policy For The Eighties,' [23] a virtual declaration of war. It pointed out:

> Foreign policy is the instrument by which people seek to assure their survival in a hostile world. War, not peace, is the norm in international affairs. For the United States of America, isolationism is impossible. Containment of the Soviet Union is not enough. Detente is dead. Survival demands a new US foreign policy. America must seize the initiative or perish. For World War III is almost over. The Soviet Union, operating under the cover of increasing nuclear superiority, is strangling the Western industrialized nations by interdicting their oil and ore supplies and is encircling the People's Republic of China. Latin America and Southern Asia are the scenes of strife of the third phase of World War III.

It presented the changes in the Caribbean as the result of "Moscow intrigues", and called for action "to control the situation" by a carrot-and-club policy - "to wed the most successful elements of the Truman Doctrine and the Alliance for Progress". Finally, it urged "revitalising the Rio Treaty and the Organization of American States; reproclaiming the Monroe Doctrine...".

President Ronald Reagan accused his predecessor of sacrificing US vital interests and resurrected the strategy of 'roll-back', 'peace through strength' and 'brinkmanship' of the Dulles era. He moved US foreign policy to a confrontationist-interventionist direction.

The first priority of US global military strategy for the 1980's was based on a major nuclear war in Europe against the Soviet Union and the socialist countries in Europe. The second priority was a major nuclear war against the revolutionary-democratic Arab nations, Afghanistan, Iran and Syria in the area of the Middle East and the Persian Gulf. And there would be 'little' wars, 'brush-fire' battles against Lebanon, Nicaragua, El Salvador, Guatemala, Angola, Ethiopia, Mozambique, etc.

Through misinformation, war hysteria, chauvinism and militaristic sentiments were whipped up, based on anti-communism and anti-sovietism, about myths of a 'worldwide conspiracy', 'a world communist threat', 'Soviet designs' and quest for 'world domination', 'red militarism', and a 'Soviet war danger'.[24]

At the same time, to create a kind of 'public apathy' about basic current questions, to undermine the anti-war movement and to prepare public opinion for a 'guns before butter' and anti-trade union policy and further economic hardships, and the inevitability of a 'future war', myths were created about 'windows of vulnerability' of the US war machine and about 'strategic inferiority' in the military sphere. Thus, the climate was created for disrupting the once recognized approximate military-strategic equality (parity between the two social systems).[25]

The Reagan administration embarked on a five-year $1.6 trillion (US) military programme,[26] including the establishment of new nuclear weapons systems, to gain superiority and to prepare the country for accepting both conventional and nuclear wars. Justifying this huge anti-people expenditure, Secretary of Defence Caspar Weinberger on April 28, 1981 said:

> Many of the resources that we need for energy, and many strategic minerals are found thousands of miles from our shores... if we are to safeguard our access, and the access to the free world to these resources, we must increase our military and naval strength.[27]

Secretary Weinberger later proposed that a significant part of the strategic forces should be capable of enduring survival, even in the cataclysmic event of a protracted nuclear war. He declared that "if the movement from 'cold war' to detente is progress", then the USA "cannot afford such progress", and Richard Pipes, Reagan's highest-ranking 'Kremlinologist' in the National Security Council reaffirmed to the *Washington Post* in April, 1982 his faith in a "winnable nuclear war". He pointed out that the losses from a nuclear holocaust, "while terrible, can be scaled down with careful planning and our determination to win a protracted conflict." Alarmingly, he referred to Nazi Germany: "What Hitler got in the 1930's, he got because he was perceived as strong and bold".[28] Deputy Chief of Staff of the US Marines Lieutenant-General Bernard Trianor told a forum at the Naval War College in Newport, Rhode Island in mid-1984 that a limited war with the Soviet Union is "an almost inevitable probability".

Contemplation of, and preparation for such diabolical plans requires an ideological under-pinning: the American people must be led to believe that communism is evil, that the Soviet Union is a real threat; that a nuclear war is 'admissible', 'winnable' and 'survivable'; that a 'limited' nuclear war will bring an easy victory over the enemy; and thus, they must be prepared to bear the heavy burdens of the arms race. This is why President Reagan embarked on an ideological crusade against the Soviet Union and communism. He described the Soviet Union as "an evil empire", and in the manner of Winston Churchill[29] and John Foster Dulles [30] told the Convention of Evangelical Christians in March 1983 that Soviet communism was "the focus of evil in the modern world" and pleaded with them not to remove themselves "from the struggle between right and wrong, good and evil". Casting the United States as the hero-nation and the Soviet Union as the villain-nation, he in good cowboy style assumed the role of a crusader with a sacred goal of saving mankind from communism. In this regard, it should be noted that before the US invasion of Grenada, the President had accused the Bishop government of exporting "the Marxist virus". And Richard Pipes told an interviewer that "detente is dead", and the Soviets had two choices: alter their socialist system or face all-out war.[31]

In the same vein, Secretary of State George Schultz stated:

> We take as part of our obligation to peace to encourage the gradual evolution of the Soviet system toward a more pluralistic political economic system.

Since the Soviets were unlikely to be blackmailed[32] into changing their system, the alternative of all-out war was no doubt being seriously contemplated. Perhaps, the President's inner convictions surfaced in an off-the-air, pre-radio broadcast when he made an allegedly jocular remark:

> My fellow Americans, I am pleased to announce I just signed legislation that will outlaw Russia forever. We begin bombing in five minutes.

Earlier, President Reagan had told out-of-town editors about the possibility of waging a limited nuclear war in Europe without it spreading to the United States.

Secretary of the Navy John Lehman in mid-1984 declared: "Who gets to shoot first will have more to do with who wins than any other factor". This is why the Reagan administration refused to agree to a nuclear arms freeze and to a "no nuclear weapons first strike" pledge or treaty, and deployed Pershing-2 and Cruise missiles in Europe. Plans are now afoot to develop anti-missile laser weapons which will be deployed in space. This is deemed necessary for a protracted nuclear war. It violates the 1967 treaty signed by the USA and the USSR to ban weapons in space.

As regards Central America and the Caribbean, deemed as an area "vital to US interests", "the Achilles heel", "the circle of crisis" and the last major "security zone", the President consistently refused to recognise socio-economic factors at the root of the problems of poverty, hunger and political instability.

Instead, in a rabble-rousing speech to the OAS in February 1982, he raised anti-Soviet, anti-Cuban and anti-Communist hysteria to new heights, and opted for military solutions. Resurrecting the Monroe Doctrine, he drew attention to the importance of the Caribbean:

> The Caribbean Region is a vital strategic and commercial artery for the United States. Nearly half of US trade, two-thirds of our imported oil, and over half of our imported strategic minerals pass through the Panama Canal or the Gulf of Mexico. Make no mistake: the well-being and security of our neighbours in this region are in our own vital interest.

And in the language of John F Kennedy,[33] the President wielded the 'big stick': "Let our friends and our adversaries understand that we will do whatever is prudent and necessary to ensure the peace and security of the Caribbean area".

In the name of security and 'vital interest', the United States expanded military aid to the civilian-military regime of El Salvador, openly supported the Somocists counter-revolutionary 'contras', mined the approaches to Nicaraguan harbours which received the condemnation of the World Court, fortified Honduras as a springboard for aggression, backed Israeli aggression against Lebanon, and invaded Grenada[34] contrary to the principles of international law and in violation of the United-Nations and OAS charters.

In contravention of the Rio Pact, the United States gave military, logistical and other support to her firmest NATO ally, Great Britain, in the Malvinas (Falklands) war, for which it was criticised at an OAS meeting and attacked by Latin American public opinion.

Cuba was threatened with intervention. The Symms Amendment, adopted by a 69 to 27 vote in the Republican-controlled Senate in mid-1982, like the Johnson Doctrine, empowered the Reagan administration to resort to all means available to the United States including the use of troops, to oppose the alleged 'Cuban threat' and to contain 'Marxist-Leninist subversion' in the region. Earlier in May 1981, former Secretary of State Alexander Haig had stated that if Cuba continued "gun running activities to Latin America, the US has not ruled out a naval blockade of Cuba". And the Santa Fe Committee declared," if propaganda fails, a war of national liberation against Cuba must be launched."

The Central American Democratic Community was created to give legitimacy to the puppet civilian-military regime of El Salvador, and to build a political 'wall' against Nicaragua.

Like Barbados and Jamaica in the Caribbean and Honduras in Central America, Washington has established client states in other regions of the world - Israel in the Middle East, South Africa in Southern Africa, Somalia in the Horn of Africa, Egypt in North Africa and the Middle East, Pakistan in Central Asia, and Thailand in South-East Asia.

The Reagan administration has embarked on a policy of cuddling the most brutal dictatorial and fascist regimes in Chile, Paraguay, South Korea, Guatemala, El Salvador, Pakistan and elsewhere. The rationale for this was provided by US ambassador to the UN, Jeanne Kirkpatrick. Her argument is "that traditional authoritarian governments are less repressive than revolutionary autocracies, that they are more susceptible to liberalisation, and that they are more compatible with US interests".

Military bases are being expanded and strengthened worldwide. In the Indian Ocean region, the United States is pressing to substitute the 'strategic consensus' idea for the 'peace zone' concept, in order to subordinate the national interests of the countries in the region towards confrontation with the Soviet Union. Plans are also being considered for the establishment of an Indian Ocean Treaty Organization (IOTO) on the NATO model.

In the Far East, in addition to the existing ANZUS treaty and the Japanese-American Defence System, a tripartite military-political alliance embracing Japan, USA and China is being added.

Attempts are being made to lure the ASEAN countries (Association of South-East Asian Countries - Indonesia, Thailand, the Philippines and Malaysia) into a 'Pacific Community', the South-East Asia Treaty Organization (SEATO) having collapsed. The aim is to achieve a 'strategic concord' between Tokyo, Seoul and the ASEAN capitals on anti-Soviet and anti-Vietnamese lines.

Washington is arming Pakistan, as a substitute for Iran under the Shah, to make it its tool in the vast area of South and South-West Asia, the Near East and the Indian Ocean basin.

A Memorandum on Mutual Understanding in the Field of Strategic Co-operation of November 30, 1981 was another step in the direction of a military pact between the USA and Zionist-racist Israel. It followed on the process started by the notorious Camp David agreement, which was to usher in an 'era of peace' and 'prosperity' in the Middle East.

Racist-fascist South Africa is deemed by President Reagan as a 'friendly country', and 'a constructive relationship' is being developed with it for a variety of pressures ranging from blackmail to destabilisation and armed aggression against the front-line states (Angola, Mozambique, Zambia, Botswana, Lesotho, Swaziland and Zimbabwe) and attacks against the African national liberation movement.

In the South Atlantic, efforts are continuing by the United States to establish the South Atlantic Treaty Organization (SATO) to embrace South Africa, Uruguay, Chile and possibly Brazil and Argentina.

At the same time, in whipping up hysteria about the 'danger from the East' and the necessity to fight the 'communist threat from within and without', the United States has sold enormous quantities of arms, with a 10-fold increase in 1980 as compared with its $1.8 billion sales in 1970. In the developing countries, military spending increased from $11.3 billion in 1960 to $77.5 billion in 1980. The arms sales serve to accomplish US global aim of hegemony and world domination, to earn super-profits for the monopolists of the arms industry, to enmesh the developing countries in a 'debt trap' and to imperil their sovereignty and independent development.[35]

Presidential Directive 138 of April 3, 1984 on the so-called combating, of 'international terrorism'[36] provides for the pre-emptive use of specially trained detachments, including regular troops, against national-patriotic and revolutionary movements and also against countries that support them. Earlier, former Assistant Secretary of State for Inter-American Affairs, Thomas Enders, charged that so-called Cuban interventionism was creating a "state of danger in the Caribbean Basin", and called for "collective action" because the "collective security" of the region was at stake. Referring to Nicaragua's alleged import of weapons and Cuban military advisers, he blustered: "Should more serious threats emerge, it is in collective security that we should seek solutions."[37] As regards El Salvador, he told the Nicaraguan Minister of Foreign Affairs, Miguel D'Escoto: "The United States is not going to allow a military triumph of the guerrillas, it has the means and the desire to do so, irrespective of the political cost."[38] And a Reagan adviser declared: "El Salvador doesn't really matter. We have to establish credibility there because we are in trouble."

Directive 138 is based on the 'Schultz Doctrine' of "preventive terrorism". It moves from condemning terrorism "passively" to "actively eradicating" it. A 'League of Terror' includes "terrorist states" such as Syria, Libya, Iran and the Korean People's Democratic Republic, and the states which support them such as the Soviet Union. Punishment would be administered by carrying through "corresponding preventive and pre-emptive actions and blows against the status constituting the 'League of Terror'."

Honduras is being fortified as a base of operations for US-sponsored state terrorism in Central America. Aid to it has increased 20 times since Presidential Directive 17 was signed in 1981. According to Senator James Susser permanent and semipermanent military facilities are being built without the approval of Congress, which "have little, if anything to do with exercises", and reminiscent of the secret military build up in South Vietnam in the 1960's for the later escalation of the war.

NO ALTERNATIVE TO PEACEFUL CO-EXISTENCE

A characteristic feature historically of class-divided countries and subjugated territories is struggle for national and social liberation. This struggle has different features - political, military, economic and ideological.

Politics has been variously described as 'who gets what, where and how' or as war by other means. Wars are either just or unjust - just: to attain and retain political power so as to carry out radical socio-economic transformations for the fulfilment of the aspirations of the working people for freedom, equality and social justice; unjust: to use chicanery, manipulation, fraud and force to acquire new spheres of influence and to maintain the Old Order.

In early times, Britain's 'vital interests' were served by war. But the weapons of war were primitive, the wars were limited and large parts of the world were sparsely populated. In 1496 John Cabot was given his royal patent by King Henry VII to "subdue, conquer and possess" all foreign lands not yet blessed by Christianity. By his two voyages of 1497 and 1498, Britain laid claim to "the mainland of North America by right of discovery" [39] In the late 1930's and early 1940's, Adolf Hitler attempted to obtain lebensraum by means of war. But like Napoleon, he and his fascist cohorts perished.

Like the Hitlerite gang, the Reagan administration is hell-bent on upsetting the military balance with a new spiral of the nuclear arms race. Having lost its superiority in strategic arms, it deployed more sophisticated Cruise and Pershing-2 missiles in Europe to gain superiority at the Eurostrategic level.[40] It has also shifted from military support to reactionary forces to direct acts of aggression as in Lebanon, Grenada and Nicaragua.

The upsetting of the military balance is justified on the rationalisation that 'military inferiority', coupled with lack of political will, caused 'lost positions' in Asia, Africa, Latin America and the Caribbean - Iran, Afghanistan, Kampuchea, Nicaragua, Panama, Grenada, etc. 'State-sponsored anti-terrorism' is also justified on the basis of 'legal right and moral duty', allegedly because 'terrorists', the appellation given to national liberation movements, and the 'intrigues' and 'aggressiveness' of Moscow (which is 'exporting revolution' and supporting 'international terrorism') are creating political instability and tensions; that tensions are threatening 'vital interests' not only in 'our region', 'our backyard', the Caribbean Basin,[41] but also in vast areas of the world. As President Reagan put it: "Today, our national security can be threatened in far-away places". The whole world has become "a theatre of hostilities". And if no action is taken, as for instance in El Salvador, it is argued that, in accordance with the domino theory, which was first linked to the war in Vietnam, the "evil empire" will be at "our doorstep". The TV documentary film 'Attack on the Americas' proclaimed:

> What is at stake is more than the freedom of our neighbours to the South, more than the oilfields of Guatemala and Mexico, more than the natural resources of our allies in the Western hemisphere. Today, El Salvador and Guatemala. Tomorrow, Honduras, Costa Rica, Belize, Venezuela, the Dominican Republic, Mexico ... the United States.[42]

This is why the Pentagon extended the 'security zone' under the Rio Pact to include the South Atlantic, and also the 'zone of responsibility' of NATO. Justifying NATO's participation with 80 planes, a British nuclear submarine and 10,000 men the US launched 'Operation Safe Passage' in early 1982 in the Gulf of Mexico, Caspar Weinberger stated that Cuba posed a threat to the United States as "in peacetime, forty four per cent of all foreign trade tonnage and forty five per cent of the crude oil imports into the United States pass through the Caribbean, and in wartime half of NATO's supplies would transit by sea from Gulf ports through the Florida Straits and onwards to Europe".

With the fervour of religious crusaders, the war-mongers argue that "good" cannot co-exist with "evil"; that no compromise can be made with the devil; that all adversaries are evil devils; and that the "evil empire" must be destroyed. So great is the threat, the argument continues, that there must be not only interference, but also pre-emptive nuclear strikes. According to the Reagan doctrine, à la the Woodrow Wilson doctrine, the USSR must be punished for not behaving well, and Cuba must be punished because of Soviet 'intervention' in Afghanistan and its 'interference' in Africa, Latin America and the Caribbean. As regards Central America, *The New York Times* wrote:

> Senior officials in the Reagan Administration say that contingency plans are being drawn for the possible use of United States combat troops in Central America if the current strategy for defeating Leftist forces in the region fails.[43]

Presidential directive 17 of December 1981 refers to "the possible use of US armed forces." And neither an 'invitation', as in the case of the US invasion of Grenada,[46] not the pretext of an external threat is necessary for intervention.[44] As Casper Weinberger said: "President Reagan would intervene if there should be anything that resembled an internal revolution in Saudi Arabia".[45] And to be free "to go all the way" with an "undeclared war", the Reagan administration is seeking legislative changes to remove restrictions embodied in the War Powers Act, the Neutrality Act and the United Nations Charter. Deputy Chief of US Naval Operations James Lyons denounced as "insidious" and "an impediment" the War Powers Act, which requires Congressional approval for commitment of armed forces overseas for more than 90 days. The Neutrality Act forbids "any military or naval expeditions or enterprises" against other countries with which "the United States is at peace".[46] And the UN Charter is based on the principles of non-intervention and the non-use of force.

The US theory of 'vital interests' runs counter to the interests of the peoples of the world. Fear of nuclear incineration and 'nuclear winter' is an ever-present pre-occupation for millions. While billions of dollars are squandered for war preparations, hundreds of millions of people particularly in the developing countries suffer from malnutrition and hunger, death from preventable diseases, illiteracy and cultural backwardness. In the developed capitalist countries, the 'welfare state' is being dismantled slowly but surely.

President Reagan's global strategy also imperils the United States itself and its real interests. The trade embargoes and 'sanctions' against the Soviet Union, Cuba, Poland, etc affect adversely the US export trade and the creation of jobs. During 1970-79 the Soviet Union obtained 60 per cent of its grain imports from the United States. In 1979, the trade turnover with a big net balance in favour of the United States was $4.5 billion. Now it is only $2.3 billion.[47] The US - USSR Trade and Economic Council estimates that government-imposed restrictions on trade with the Soviet Union cost American companies $10 billion a year. So important was trade to the American farmers that even President Reagan was forced to remove the ban on grain sales to the USSR which had been imposed by the Carter administration; he was also forced as a result of pressures from subsidiaries of US companies in England and France and other European companies to remove the embargo on the sale of oil pipes to the USSR in exchange for gas.

The wasteful expenditure of trillions of dollars for the arms race sacrifices investment for economic growth and jobs, cuts social programmes, distorts technological progress and hits the high technology sector. Columbia University Professor Buymour Melman, co-chairman of the peace organization SANE told the Dellums' Congressional Committee hearings that the military build-up was "looting the means of production" by diverting capital investment into weapons of mass destruction. He pointed out: "Seven per cent of military outlays from fiscal 1981-86, $100 billion, is equal to the cost of rehabilitating the United States' steel industry so that it is again the most efficient in the world". The Navy's F-18 fighter programme, he said, at a cost of $34 billion, equals "the cost of modernising America's machine-tool stock to bring it to the average level of Japan's."[48]

And even the much-touted democratic values (bourgeois) are at stake. As Henry Salvatori, an early backer of Reagan's political career and member of his Kitchen Cabinet, put it: "We have to have a new consensus. We have to cement together a sense of social order. In the history of man, everyone has talked about expanding rights, having more and more freedom. But we have found that if you let people do what they want to do, you have chaos. We can't restore moral values, that's hopeless. What we have to do is restructure society, get minimum standards of respect and order. Frankly we need a more authoritarian state."[49]

The tensions and political instability in the capitalist world are due not to 'Moscow intrigues' and 'terrorism', but to the general crisis of capitalism which, coupled with the scientific and technological revolution, reproduces its inherent contradictions on an ever-growing scale at the centre and the periphery. The crisis in the 'Third World' is due not to 'Soviet expansionsism', but to underdevelopment and blatant exploitation and drain of resources[50] under a dependent/distorted capitalist way of 'development' fostered by imperialism's Point Four [51] and Marshall [52] plans under President Truman, Alliance for Progress [53] under Presidents Kennedy and Johnson and the Caribbean Basin Initiative (mini-Marshall Plan) under President Reagan - a way of 'development' which leads to a vicious circle of backwardness, poverty, instability and further dependence. This in turn leads to an intensification of the class and national liberation struggles of the peoples fighting heroically to satisfy their aspirations for a better life.

In this era of transition from capitalism to socialism, the historical process cannot be reversed by war. Militarism in the past did not succeed in stopping the inexorable tide of history. The 'roll-back'[54] strategy did not attain its objective after World

War II of "liberating the captive states", what Winston Churchill called "the ancient capitals of Europe".

In an attempt to restore colonialism in Indonesia and Indochina, the Dutch and French imperialists respectively were disastrously defeated in the battlefields. General Charles De Gaulle was brought out of forced retirement and given extraordinary political powers to keep Algeria French. But in the end, he was forced to proceed against those who put him in power and to grant independence to Algeria. The anti-colonial national liberation wars in the former Portuguese colonies of Angola, Mozambique and Guinea Bissau rocked the foundations of fascist Portugal, leading to a revolution there, which in turn influenced the granting of independence to its colonial territories in Africa.

British and French imperialism suffered a severe political defeat in Egypt in 1956, when the British-French-Israeli military aggression and the Eisenhower/Dulles 'brinkmanship' proved a fiasco.

President Truman dismissed General Douglas MacArthur, who during the Korean war (1950-53) had advocated invading China and using atomic bombs. His Cold-War-mongering notwithstanding, Truman knew, as a realist, that the communists had come to power in China in 1949 despite tremendous US military and economic assistance to the corrupt Chiang kai-Shek regime, and that MacArthur's reckless military adventure would lead the United States into a quagmire, as happened later in Vietnam under successive US administrations until President Richard Nixon, the rabid Cold War warrior and anti-Communist witch-hunter of the McCarthy era, under pressure, sued for peace.

The historical rivalry between capitalism and socialism cannot be solved by war. World War II with only conventional weapons led to the slaughter of nearly 50 million people, 20 million in the Soviet Union alone. Two atomic bombs dropped at Hiroshima and Nagasaki in Japan towards the end of World War II led to death and grave immediate and genetic injury to hundreds of thousands. Today there are over 50,000 nuclear warheads, each with a thousand times more explosive power than those in 1945. Like the legendary sword of Damocles life literally hangs by a thread. The present stockpile of nuclear weapons can destroy the world many times over. And with the present high level of sophistication of nuclear weaponry, there is always the danger of an accidental nuclear conflagration. In recent years, according to authoritative sources, the US early warning systems have sounded many false alarms of a nuclear attack.

The 'nuclear deterrence' and 'balance of terror' concepts have not proved efficacious in ensuring international security. In practice, they have led in the West to larger increments of weaponry with greater destructive and lethal force, and to the creation of a climate of intimidation, terror and fear.

The 'balance of terror', the unbridled arms race and 'military superiority' for 'self security', with total disregard for the interests of other peoples and countries, must be replaced by a totally different kind of security at international and regional levels. To attain a genuine balance of security, it is necessary to reduce the levels of military confrontation while maintaining parity: an equilibrium between the military strength of socialism and imperialism, of the USSR and USA, of the Warsaw Pact and NATO alliances. Instead of 'self security', there should be emphasis on 'equal security', 'general security' and 'collective security'. Instead of 'balance of terror', confrontation and military intimidation, there is need for a real recipe for peace. This means conducting international relations on the basis of peaceful co-existence in all its various aspects: political detente, normalisation of inter-state relations, economic co-operation and military detente. It means conducting economic relations also between developing and developed countries not on the basis of a feigned 'interdependence of nations' and the 'law of the jungle', but on the principles of peaceful co-existence, mutual benefit, good neighbourliness and co-operation.

In the 1970's, the Decade of detente, many beneficial agreements in the cause of peace and security were reached. Following the Partial Test Ban Treaty of 1963, the Soviet-French Declaration of 1966, the Outer Space Treaty of 1967, and Willie Brandt's 'Ostpolitik' and treaties signed in the early 1970's by the Federal Republic of Germany with the USSR, Poland, the

German Democratic Republic and Czechoslovakia, the following measures furthered the principles of peaceful co-existence, detente and 'equal security':

- Antarctic Treaty (1970);

- Agreement on Measures to Reduce the Risk of Outbreak of Nuclear War Between the USSR and the USA (1971);

- Basic Principles of Mutual Relations Between the Union of Soviet Socialist Republics and the United States of America, signed in Moscow (May 1972);

- Agreement on the Prevention of Nuclear War (1973);

- Helsinki Final Act (1975) of the Conference on Security and Co-operation in Europe; 1975;

- Treaty on the Non-Proliferation of Nuclear Weapons;

- Treaty on the Prohibition of the Emplacement of Nuclear Weapons and Other Weapons of Mass Destruction on the Sea-Bed and the Ocean Floor and in the Subsoil Thereof;

- Convention on the Prohibition of the Development, Production and Stockpiling of Bacteriological (Biological) and Toxic Weapons and on Their Destruction;

- Convention on the Prohibition of Military or any other Hostile Use of Environmental Modification Techniques (1980);

- Convention on Prohibition or Restrictions on the Use of Certain Conventional Weapons, opened for signing on April 4, 1981.

The basis of The Basic Principles of Mutual Relations set out that the USSR and the USA "will proceed from the common determination that in the nuclear age there is no alternative to conducting their mutual relations but on the basis of peaceful co-existence."[55]

The Agreement on the Prevention of Nuclear War, signed by Presidents Nixon and Brezhnev in 1973, committed the USSR and the USA to:

> ... act in such a manner as to prevent the development of situations capable of causing a dangerous exacerbation of their relations, as to avoid military confrontations, and as to exclude the outbreak of nuclear war between them and between either of the Parties and other countries.[56]

The Helsinki Final Act led to political detente, a favourable international climate, and lifted the dread of a nuclear holocaust. It also caused a shift in US foreign policy. The 1974 report of the Congressional Committee on Foreign Affairs, 'Human Rights in the World Community: A Call for US Leadership', stated that previous US policy had "led the United States into embracing governments which practice torture and unabashedly violate every human rights guarantee pronounced by the world community",[57] thus damaging both American prestige and its long term interests. And the 1974 and 1976 reports of the Commission on United States-Latin American Relations, headed by Sol Linowitz, in 'The Americas In A Changing World', pointed out that "covert US involvement in the domestic politics of Latin America such as occurred more recently in Chile is indefensible and should be ended."[58] With the repeal of the Internal Security Act of 1950, McCarthyism was officially buried.

In keeping with this policy shift to detente, the Carter administration at first was more amenable to observing the principles of international law. At a UN Human Rights Commission meeting, its delegate admitted and criticized US complicity in the overthrow of the Allende government.

President Carter signed the US Panama treaty recognizing Panama's partial control of the Canal Zone[59] and full sovereignty by the year 2000; did not send 'a peace-keeping force' to Nicaragua in 1979 after a negative vote by the OAS, and along with Soviet President Brezhnev initialed the SALT II Treaty. Instead of resorting to armed intervention to rescue American hostages seized by the Khomeini government of Iran, he utilized the United Nations and the World Court.[60] And the OAS lifted its blockade of Cuba, embraced ideological pluralism and in October 1979 called on all states to recognise the Caribbean as a zone of peace and to devote all the efforts, in appropriate regional and international forums, to the advancement of this concept. The Latin American countries also elaborated a Charter on the Economic Rights and Duties of States, on the creation of equality in international economic relations and a Code of Behaviour for multinational corporations[61] The Declaration of Tlatelolco (Mexico) of 1974 gave expression to the principles of non-interference, equality, rejection of the use of force and coercion, and also to the right of each state to choose its own political, economic and social system.[62]

When spokesmen of the Reagan administration claim that detente is "dead" and that it did not signify progress, they are obviously referring to the interests not of the people but of the capitalist ruling class. Political detente must be restored. And to avoid military confrontation and to exclude the outbreak of nuclear war, there must be military detente. The arms race must be ended. This has been pointed out since 1978 by the First Special Session on Disarmament (SSOD-1). Its Final Declaration pronounced: "Mankind is faced with a choice: we must halt the arms race and proceed to disarmament or face annihilation". A nuclear war would lead to total destruction of human civilization and possibly also to the destruction of all life on earth.

So vital and urgent was the issue that the United Nations declared the 1980's as the 'Decade of Disarmament'. Pinpointing the gravity of the situation, UN Secretary General

Xavier Perez de Cuellar in 1982 told the Second Special Session on Disarmament (SSOD-2):

> All decision-makers know that, by its very nature, a nuclear war cannot remain limited ... An all-out nuclear confrontation would affect the entire world, the entire ecosystem. Vital parts of the ozone layer, which protects the earth from ultra-violet radiation, would be destroyed, with catastrophic consequences for human beings, animals and vegetation. All services essential to sustain life would be detrimentally affected. The infrastructure of civilization would be shattered... There is no possibility of winning a nuclear war in any conceivable sense of the word "win"; the end of civilization could hardly be anyone's victory. A very apt description of the consequences of a nuclear confrontation is: "The living will envy the dead."[63]

Former CIA Deputy Director Hubert Scoville, now head of the Arms Control Association said that the use of nuclear weapons in Europe would mean: "no Europe left, no Soviet Union left, no United States left."[64]

Militarisation and military confrontation is no guarantee of security. The only sane alternative is peaceful co-existence. This means embarking on a programme which includes the principles of economic and political independence, relations of friendship and mutually beneficial co-operation on the basis of equality between countries of different socio-economic systems. The urgent global problems pertaining to natural resources, energy, food, environment, dangerous contagious diseases, fresh water and arable land are crying out for solutions. With co-operation, many problems could be solved. The war-time anti-Hitler coalition of eleven capitalist states and one socialist state served the interests of all. Such co-operation must again be instituted for the sake of humankind.

In the military sphere, military detente and disarmament should be sought through:

-   a non-nuclear-first-strike treaty as proposed by the Soviet Union and approved by the United Nations General Assembly by a vote of 82 to 19;

-   respect and observance [65] of the Strategic Arms Limitation Treaty, SALT-1; ratification by the US Congress of SALT-2 signed by Presidents Brezhnev and Carter in 1979, and commencement of work on SALT-3;

-   a nuclear arms freeze (already approved by the United Nations and supported by three-quarters of the American people);

-   a treaty outlawing the use of force in outer space and from outer space with regard to the Earth;

-   a non-aggression pact between NATO and the Warsaw Treaty Organization and total renunciation by both alliances of all types of nuclear missiles, medium-range and tactical, deployed in or near Europe;

-   removal from the arsenals of states of chemical and bacteriological and other mass destruction weapons;

-   a halt to the testing of nuclear arms, which encourages the arms race, promotes the development of nuclear weaponry and destabilises the global strategic situation;

-   the ratification of the 1974 Soviet-US treaty on the limitation of underground nuclear explosives for peaceful purposes;

-   the creation of nuclear-free peace zones;

-   curtailment of the CIA's 'covert action' powers and strict scrutiny of its activities, as was done after its bugging of Watergate. Even President Truman in 1963 had called for curbs on its activities;[66]

- framing of a code of conduct and international law for the curtailment and eventual elimination of economic warfare through sanctions, embargoes and boycotts;

- strengthening the United Nations [67] peace-keeping role for multilateral security;

- diversion of funds from the arms race to development;

- engagement in a global round of negotiations under the United Nations for a New International Economic Order and equitable international economic relations;

- ratification of the Law of the Sea by the United States,

- instituting a Code of Conduct for the transnational corporations;

- establishing a New International Information order in the struggle against mis-information and cultural imperialism.

Psychological warfare based on the myth of 'strategic lag' must give way to fair ideological competition. US sponsorship of 'state terrorism' must be replaced by recognition of, and respect for, the principles of international law governing inter-state relations. Economic aid [68] such as the Caribbean Basin Initiative (CBI), must not be tied to a military programme, and used as a weapon to undermine the political independence of sovereign states.

A policy of political and ethical realism of the Santa Fe Committee must not mean for Latin America and the Caribbean the abandonment of the doctrine of ideological pluralism and human rights for the embrace of ruthless dictators in the guise of fighting 'terrorism'; "a vigorously and equitably applied human rights programme" must not become "America's wonder weapon against the Soviet Union, its satellites and surrogates".

Those who in the Reagan administration call today's freedom fighters 'terrorists' have forgotten that the 13 British North American colonies had been helped by Jacobean France in their war of independence (Britain also aided liberator Simon Bolivar in his struggle against Spanish colonialism); that the "American revolution", as stated by Millen Chamberlain, "was not a quarrel between two peoples ... it was a strife between two parties, the conservatives in both countries as one party, and the liberals in both countries as the other party", [69] As historian Charles Beard put it: "The contest in America was only the counterpart of the heroic struggle led by Russell, Cobden, Bright and Gladstone at home to establish the dominion of the English mill owners over Crown, Clergy, and landed aristocracy"; that one of the founding fathers, democrat Thomas Jefferson, who had resided in France and was a disciple of Voltaire, Diderot and Rousseau, believed that "a little rebellion now and then is a good thing..." and that "the tree of liberty must be refreshed from time to time with the blood of tyrants". [70] On the other hand, a retired Justice John Reeve had established a society for the protection of private property against levellers and republicans. Today, Reeve's levellers and republicans are Reagan's Marxist-Leninists and communists who are deemed 'terrorists'. Forgotten is the role of the CIA in the overthrow of the Arbenz Government in 1954, and US history of interventions, rape of democracy, creation of client states and puppet regimes, and collective security for the purpose of maintaining colonial and neo-colonial dependency.

The real interests of the peoples demand as a first priority the struggle for world peace. But peace is not an abstraction; it is dialectically linked with liberation and development. The struggle for peace must be associated with the struggle for national and social liberation and for development. In this regard, unity and solidarity are essential. The three world revolutionary streams - the socialist community, the national liberation movements in the 'Third World' and the working class and democratic forces in the capitalist world - must work in the closest co-operation. And militant solidarity must be extended to counter imperialist destabilisation and aggression.

The struggle for world peace must be intensified. The foremost human right - the right to life - is threatened. Life can be safe-guarded by co-operation, not confrontation. The three world's political forces - the socialist, non-aligned and capitalist - whatever their differences, have pronounced in favour of peace.

The 26th Congress of the Communist Party of the Soviet Union (CPSU) stated:

> To safeguard peace - no task is more important on the international plane for our Party, for our people and, for that matter, for all the peoples of the world ... Not war preparations that doom the peoples to a senseless squandering of their national and spiritual wealth, but consolidation of peace - that is the clue to the future.

President Konstantin Chernanko declared: "No aim is more urgent than to safeguard the human race, and no task more important than to see to it that the dreams of lasting peace, of welfare and prosperity, do not remain a splendid utopia. The road to this goal is not easy, but it is obvious - to renounce confrontation and to embark firmly on detente, co-operation, and peaceful co-existence, and to begin a radical reduction of armaments on the principles of equality and equal security." [71] The Soviet leader further pointed out that if nuclear states pledged not to use nuclear weapons first and accepted a qualitative and quantitative freeze of nuclear arsenals, which did not call for complicated negotiations, there would be a radical change for the better in the world.

Indira Gandhi, Prime Minister of India and current chairperson of the Non-Aligned Movement stated:

> We are against militarism and any forms of domination. We are in favour of a peaceful resolution of disagreements and uphold the cause of co-operation in the interests of the whole of humanity. We believe in co-existence. The world is large enough for all of us to exist, irrespective or our political convictions, religious and racial affiliations, but it is not large enough for us to survive in a war involving nuclear weapons.[72]

Indira Gandhi and five other heads-of-governments - President Miguel de la Madrid of Mexico, President Julius Nyerere of Tanzania, Prime Minister Andreas Papandreou of Greece, President Raul Alfonsin of Argentina, and Prime Minister Olof Palme of Sweden - made a Peace Appeal to nuclear powers, urging that a nuclear war must not be allowed to occur in any form, the ending of the stockpiling of nuclear weapons and the freezing of nuclear arsenals.

President Ronald Reagan told the UN Second Special Session On Disarmament (SSOD-2) in 1982:

> I speak today as a citizen both of the United States and of the world.
> I come with the heartfelt wishes of my people for peace bearing honest proposals and looking for genuine progress.

The US President had also said that whatever the differences between the USA and the USSR, there are "common interests and the foremost among them is to avoid, and reduce the level of arms."[73]

Richard Nixon, who contributed to political detente in the 1970's, declared that he saw no alternative to peaceful co-existence. Venturing a definition, he said: "We can call this peaceful competition... it is better than the alternatives of either sterile confrontation or nuclear conflict".[74] He wanted relations between the USSR and the USA to be put on the basis of a code of conduct. This view is now shared by a large section of the spokesmen of the US ruling class, who take not an adventuristic but a realistic position.

Rhetoric must be translated into reality. The 'politics of adventurism' must give way to the 'politics of realism'. World public opinion must be mobilised to pressure the political leaders to put words into deeds, halt the arms race, ensure peace and serve the real interests of all.

NOTES

[1] Paper given at XII Congress of International Association of Democratic Lawyers, Athens, 15 October 1984.

[2] Referring to CIA coups in Iran and Guatemala in 1953 and 1954 respectively, CIA director Allan Dulles wrote: "Where there begins to be evidence that a county is slipping and Communist take-over is threatened ... we can't wait for an engraved invitation to come and give aid". (Victor Marchetti and John D Marks, *The CIA and the Cult of Intelligence*, Knopf, 1974, p. 26).

[3] A Lebedev, S Gribanov, 'Lenin's Concept of Peaceful Co-existence and Present Day World', *International Affairs*, Moscow, 5/1984, p. 17.

[4] The US Secretary of State, John Quincy Adams, in his doctrine of Manifest Destiny of 1819 observed that the absorption of all North America was ..." as much a law of nature ... as that the Mississippi should flow to the sea". It was, he held "a physical, moral and political absurdity" that European colonies "should exist permanently contiguous to a great, powerful and rapidly-growing nation". (Quoted in Julius W Pratt, *A History of United States Foreign Policy* Prentice Hall, Inc. N J 1965, p. 75.

[5] Some of the principles of the bourgeois Monroe Doctrine had a progressive significance for that period. The Americans pointed out that while the European kings and emperors took the doctrine of inalienable allegiance as a basis for human society and regarded the Latin American liberation struggle as a rebellion against their legitimate sovereignty, the "US doctrine was based on the principle of inalienable law", and the anti-colonial liberation struggle was viewed "as an expression of natural law". (See Nikolai Bolkhovitinov, 'The Monroe Doctrine', *Pan-Americanism: Its Essence and Evolution*,' Moscow, 1982, p. 29.

[6] President Theodore Roosevelt stated that "the adherence of the United States to the Monroe Doctrine may force the United States, however reluctantly ... to the exercise of international police power".

[7] See William Appleman Williams, 'American Intervention in Russia 1917-20', *Containment and Revolution*, edited by David Horowitz, Beacon Press, Boston, 1967, pp. 27-31.

[8] Cited in Julius Pratt, op. cit., p. 370.

[9] Quoted in D F Fleming, *The Cold War and its Origins*, Doubleday & Co., Inc. New York, 1961, p. 437.

[10] Quoted in Robert Armstrong, 'By What Right? US Foreign Policy 1945-83' NACLA, New York, November/December 1983, p. 7.

[11] Semyon Gonionsky, 'The Rio De Janeiro Act', *Pan Americanism*, op. cit., p. 71.

[12] Such was their vassal status that US laws - the Law of Reciprocal Aid of 1949 and the Law of Mutual Security of 1951 - were also applicable to them. Under the first Mutual Defence Assistance (MDA) agreement between Ecuador and the USA,- in January 1952, Ecuador agreed "to facilitate the production and transfer ... of ... strategic materials required by the United States" and to co-operate in the blocking of trade with the socialist world, and the United States government agreed "to make available... equipment, material, services and other military assistance designed to promote the defence and maintain the peace of the Western Hemisphere". Edwin Lieuwen, *Arms and Politics in Latin America*, Frederick Praeger, New York, 1960, p. 201.

[13] Derived from Senator Joseph McCarthy, who whipped up a campaign of anti-communist hysteria; he charged that the State Department was infested with communists. The campaign led to the invasion of privacy and persecution (blacklisting) of 'subversives'. An investigation against him later revealed shady deals and financial transactions and activities for such special interests groups as the real estate, sugar and China lobbies, and led to his condemnation by the Senate by a vote 67 to 22 in December 2, 1954.

[14] James West, 'Who Is Preparing For War And Who Seeks Peace', *World Marxist Review*, London, April 1982, p. 26.

[15] Nelson Rockefeller, in a confidential letter to President Eisenhower ,declared: ... virtually all our natural rubber, manganese, chromium and tin, as well as substantial proportions of our zinc, copper and oil and a third or more of the lead and aluminium we need come from abroad... By the use of economic aid we succeeded in getting access to Iranian oil and we are now well established in the economy of that country. The strengthening of our economic position in Iran has enabled us to acquire control over her entire foreign policy and in particular to make her join the Baghdad pact. At the present time the Shah would not dare even to make any changes in his Cabinet without consulting our Ambassador."

[16] The Johnson Doctrine was similar to the Lyttleton (British Colonial Secretary Oliver Lyttleton) Doctrine which, in connection with the forcible removal in October 1953 of the first popularly-elected government of the People's Progressive Party, had stated: "Her Majesty's Government is not willing to allow a communist state to be organized within the British Commonwealth" - See Cheddi Jagan, *The West on Trial*, Seven Seas Publishers, Berlin, 1980, p. 129.

[17] President Eisenhower had justified this intervention on the ground: "...So when the United States votes $400 million to help that war, we are not voting a give-away programme. We are voting for the cheapest way we can to prevent the

occurrence of something that would be of a most terrible significance to the United States of America, our security, our power and ability to get certain things we need from the riches of the Indochinese territory and from Southeast Asia."

[18] D F Fleming, op. cit., p. 781.

[19] George Ball, former US Under Secretary of State and one-time Chairman of the big investment banking firm, Lehman Bros., stated: "The multi-national US corporation is ahead of, and in conflict with, existing world political organizations represented by the nation-state. Major obstacles to the multi-national corporation are evident in Western Europe, Canada and a good part of the developing world". (Quoted in Cheddi Jagan's *The West on Trial*, p. 399).

E H Carr, *World Without Borders*, p. 225, wrote that "... the self-determination of small nations was incompatible with unbridled economic power and complete economic interdependence". (Mai Volkov, 'The "Interdependence of Nations" and Neo-colonialism' *Social Sciences*, 1/1982, p. 128).

[20] From 1945 to 1980, US private investments increased tenfold from $4 billion to $40 billion. Total investments increased in 1980 in the developing countries by $18.3 billion, and in the world by $26.7 billion, making a world total of $213.5 billion.

According to 'Transnationals in the Capitalist World' (*World Marxist Review*, April 1982, p. 75). "Throughout the 1970's, US transnationals increased their investments abroad from $78 billion to $193 billion, or by 150 per cent, while the mass of net-profit went up from $9 billion to $38 billion, or more than 300 per cent. It has doubled only in the past three years. Their profitability (ratio earnings to invested capital) went up from 12 per cent to 21 per cent. This is an inidcator which is, as a rule, much higher for the subsidiaries of US and other transnationals than it is for local companies, even in the developed countries."

[21] According to the Raw Materials and Foreign Policy compiled by the US International Economic Studies Institute, "by the mid-1970's the United States had turned from a net exporter of raw materials into a net importer... In 1976 the United States imported 100 per cent of the columbium and strontium consumed in the country, 99% of the manganese, 98% of the cobalt, 95% of the bauxite, etc... in 1985 nearly 50% of the country's raw material requirements will be met by imports". (Karen Brutents, *The Newly Free Countries in the Seventies*, Progress Publishers, Moscow, 1983, p. 25).

[22] Y Gudkov, 'Same Old Policy', *New Times*, Moscow, 20/1980, p. 23.

[23] The Committee of Santa Fe, *A New Inter-American Policy For The Eighties*, Council for Inter-American Security, Inc., Washington D. C., p. 2.

[24] Senator William Proxmire used strong language to describe CIA reports as statistical mirage, rubbish, nonsense, fake and fraud. He charged that those wanting a further inflation of military expenditure by the USA and NATO were following the recommendation of John Foster Dulles: "To make a nation bear the burden of keeping powerful armed forces, you have to create a semblance of a threat from outside."

[25] Western leaders, including US Presidents from Nixon to Carter. Former West German Chancellor Schmidt and others, had recognized the existence of parity. But the US militarist 'Committee on the Present Danger' in 1979, though admitting "parity in essence" between the USA and the USSR, alleged that the correlation of forces was changing in favour of the Soviet Union.

[26] In the 35 years from 1946 to 1980, the US spent 2,000,000 million dollars on military purposes.

[27] Quoted in John Pittman, 'Detente: The Only Sane Option', *Political Affairs*, New York, May 1982, p. 7.

[28] Tim Wheeler, 'Growing Challenge to Nuclear Power', *Political Affairs*, May 1982, p.9.

[29] Winston Churchill in his Fulton Speech in 1946 had called for joint British/ American action in bringing about through the preponderance of military power "good understanding" namely, a showdown with the USSR, the leaders of which he had always previously regarded "as murderers and ministers of hell".

[30] John Foster Dulles condemned containment as "negative, futile and immoral", because it left "countless human beings to a despotism and Godless terrorism" - Robert Armstrong, op.cit.

[31] Tim Wheeler, op. cit., p. 9.

[32] President Konstantin Chernenko declared: "The organizers of the so-called crusade against the USSR and other socialist countries would like to bring us to our knees. That will never happen". *Whence The Threat to Peace*, Moscow, 1984, p. 95.

[33] President John F Kennedy had stated: "Let every nation know, whether it wishes us well or ill, that we shall pay any price, bear any burden, meet any hardship, support any friend, oppose any foes, in order to assure the survival and success of liberty. This we pledge". (Cited in Robert Armstrong, op. cit., p. 12).

[34] As regards the US invasion of Grenada, the *Patriot* (India), February 22, 1984 states: "The brazen excuse was, again, an alleged threat to 'vital US interests'. An official paper of the Reagan Administration had said: The Middle East may be the petroleum pump, but for the United States the Atlantic is the oil line and the Caribbean has been increasingly infested with a cancer that threatens to choke off the oil and ore vital to the survival of the United States. (Particularly noted in this context was the situation of Grenada on the northern edge of the Tobago Passage, through which super tankers from Arabia and Africa move.)"

[35] According to *New Times*, (Supplement 1982, p. 14): "The arms race is a regular gold mine for the munitions monopolies. Economists have estimated that in the civilian industries the rate of profit is 8-12 per cent, while military orders show a rate of 30-40 per cent. Nor is that the limit. One of the US Senate committees which examined the state of things in 131 monopolies of the military-industrial complex established that 94 of them had made a net profit of 50 per cent; 49, more than 100 per cent; 22, over 200 per cent; three, about 500 per cent; and one

corporation, 2,000 per cent of the invested capital." And John Pittman (*Political Affairs*, N.Y. May 1982 p. 6 stated: "In its 1979 issue, the French journal *Defence National* calculated the profits on war material of ten leading suppliers of the Pentagon during the two decades, 1955 1975. Of profits realized during that period, Boeing got $18 billion; General Dynamics, $14 billion; North American, $13.3 billion; United Aircraft, $11.6 billion; General Motors, $10.5 billion; Douglas, $8.5 billion; American Telephone and Telegraph, $7.1 billion; Martin-Marietta, $6.6 billion; McDonnell, $5.7 billion; Sperry Rand, $5.6 billion - a total of $100.9 billion for the ten companies."

[36] See Audrei Grackyov, 'Preventive Terrorism,' *Moscow News*, No 27, 1984, p. 6.

[37] *The Daily Gleaner*, Jamaica, December 23, 1981.

[38] Jenny Pearce, *Under the Eagle*, Latin America Bureau, London, 1981, p. 250.

[39] R. Palme Dutt, *The Crisis of Britain and the British Empire* Lawrence and Wishart, London 1957, p. 20.

[40] The Soviets feel that the deployment of cruise and Pershing 2 missiles in West Germany and revolutionists calls in certain quarters (CDU/CSU) for West German frontiers as of December 31, 1937 is a violation of USSR-FRG treaty of August 12, 1970 which recorded that they "regard it as an important aim of their policy to maintain international peace and achieve relaxation of tension ... peace in Europe can be maintained only if no one encroaches on the present borders."

[41] A Reagan adviser James Theberge writing about Central America in *Commonsense* (Spring 1980) urged: ".... The United States may find it necessary to enforce a political solution if the alternative is civil war and the capture of a power by another Marxist regime in Central America."

[42] Jenny Pearce, op. cit., p. 107.

[43] Quoted in Yuri Gudkov, 'Ready To Go All The Way' *New Times*, Moscow 33/84, p. 18.

[44] Se Viktor Pashchuk, 'Revolutionary Cuba and Inter-American Relations' *Pan American*, op. cit. p. 113. Article 52 of the UN Charter was breached with the invasion of Grenada by the United States and the OECS member states. (Organization of Eastern Caribbean States comprising St Lucia, Grenada, Dominica, Antigua, St/ Kitts/Nevis, St. Vincent, Montserrat). The Reagan administration claimed that the US-led invasion was based on an invitation from the OECS. Even if that was true, the fact remains that the regional body had not yet received official status by the United Nations.

[45] Yuri Gudkov, op. cit., p. 21.

[46] Ibid, p. 19.

[47] Genrikh Bazhenov, 'The Sanctions A Failure', *New Times*, Moscow, 33/84, p. 5.

[48] Tim Wheeler, op. cit., p. 9.

[49] Cited in 'Reagan Policy in Crisis: Will the Empire Strike Back?' NACLA, July-August 1981.

[50] Imperialist plunder of 'Third World' countries is estimated at $120-130,000 million (about one-third of their exports and 8-10% of their GNP), taking into account profits from investments, debt payments, losses from unequal international trade, the West's protectionist policies, freight, science and technology, brain drain and inflation.

According to John Pitman. 'Detente: The Only Sane Option'. (*Political Affairs*, op. cit.) 178 US "leading corporations obtained thirty eight per cent of their profits in 1964 from operations in foreign countries, but forty seven per cent in 1969 and sixty nine per cent in 1971. With the shift in the sources of profits the transnationals have increased their role in the making of policy".

The *World Marxist Review*, April 1982, p. 75 in 'Transnationals in the Capitalist World', states "... in 1979 the net profits of fifty major international monopolies exceeded $1 billion. Altogether, in the second half of the 1970's, these giants of transnational business increased their profits by two hundred and forty per cent".

Anne Gurley in 'The Five Most Notorious Anti-Labour Regimes' (*Political Affairs*, N.Y. May 1982, p. 28) writes: "Ernest De Maio contrasts profits of the monopolies in capitalist countries with the developing countries [World Trade Union Movement, WFTU, 1981, No. 1.] At the beginning of the seventies the profit rate for capitalist countries was 10.5 per cent and for developing countries 21 per cent. At the end of the seventies for capitalist countries it was 11.0 per cent and for developing countries 25.2 per cent. From 1970 to 1978 the US multi-nationals repatriated profits of $39.7 billion [cited in *World Trade Union Movement*, 1981, No.7] Multinationals based in other countries repatriated $62.5 billion".

Mai Volkov, 'The "Interdependence of Nations" and Neo-colonialism', *Social Sciences*, Moscow, 1/1982, p. 131 states: "According to UN data, the young states have to pay annually to transnational corporations about 10 billion dollars only for utilising their technologies. If we add to this indirect expenses involved in acquiring modern technical means, then the overall contribution gathered by transnationals from the developing world probably amounts to from thirty to fifty billion dollars every year".

Abelardo L. Valdez, former US Aid Assistant Administrator for Latin America and the Caribbean, told the Inter-American Affairs Sub-Committee of the US House Foreign Affairs Committee in February 1979: "The Region provides many of the resources most vital to our economy. It is our third largest market after Western Europe and Japan purchasing $20 billion in US exports. Our direct private investment exceeds $27 billion, or 82 per cent of our investment in the entire developing world. It earns $4 billion a year".

[51] *The Times* (London), referring to Point Four, on March 3, 1952 wrote: ".... what is called economic aid is merely a cheaper form of military assistance" (p. 295); and the Third Annual Report of the Colombo Plan, the British counterpart of Point Four for Pakistan, British Borneo, India, Ceylon and Malaysia noted:

"Most Colombo countries have taken special measures to improve the climate for foreign investment".

[52] The Marshal Plan's objective was explained by the Harriman Report in 1947: "The interests of the United States in Europe cannot be measured simply in economic terms. It is also strategic and political". (Quoted in R. Palme Dutt, op. cit., p. 112)

[53] In August 1963, the US House of Representatives made an amendment to the law on foreign aid, according to which not less than fifty per cent of the means assigned to the Alliance For Progress programme was to be used for the direct financing of the private sector in Latin America". Yuri Elytutin, "The Alliance For Progress and Its Reactionary Essence", *Pan Americanism*, op. cit. P. 100.

[54] President Yuri Andropov warned: "Those who encroached on the integrity of our state, its independence and our system found themselves on the garbage heap of history", and that "it is impossible to reverse the course of history".

[55] John Pittman, op. cit., p. 3.

[56] Ibid

[57] Quoted in Jenny Pearce, op. cit., p. 108.

[58] Ibid., p. 109.

[59] "In 1903, when Colombia refused to lease to the United States the territory which it needed for building a canal across the Isthmus of Panama. Washington engineered a 'revolution' in that territory, delcared it a republic and forced the new government to sign a shackling treaty putting the entire future canal zone under US jurisdiction" (Yuri Gvozde, *Under the Cover of Inter-American Solidarity*, Novosti Press Agency Publishing House, Moscow, 1983, p. 8.)

[60] When Nicaragua accused the USA before the World Council for the CIA mining of the approaches to its harbours, the United States refused to recognize its jurisdication for a period of two years.

[61] Anatoli Glinkin, Viktor Lunin, Boris Martynov, 'The New International Situation and the Crisis of the Inter-American System' *Pan-Americanism*, op. cit., p. 128.

[62] Ibid., p. 143. The 1976 San Jose protocol of reforms of the OAS excluded from the so called security zone of the inter-American system both Greenland and large areas of the high seas.

[63] Disarmament, United Nations, N.Y. 1982, pp. 10-11.

[64] Quoted by Arthur Zipser in *World Marxist Review*, June 1982, p. 97.

[65] Reagan's chief adviser, Edwin Meese, cynically stated: "We feel there is no legal or moral commitment to abide by SALT-1", although it had been signed by a US President and ratified by the US Congress (James West, op. cit., p. 25).

[66] President Truman wrote: "... There are some searching questions that need to be answered. I ... would like to see the CIA be restored to its original assignment as the intelligence arm of the President, and whatever else it can properly perform in that special field - and that its operation duties be terminated or properly used elsewhere... There is something about the way the CIA has been functioning that is casting a shadow over our historic position and I feel that we need to correct it". (David Wise and Thomas B. Rose, *The Invisible Government*, Random House, N.Y. 1964, p. 249). The CIA was restricted after 'Watergate,' but was unleashed under the Reagan administration.

[67] In 1950, the United States with a majority in the United Nations railroaded a resolution condemning the People's Democratic Republic of Korea as an aggressor and giving a UN label and cover to the US interventionist forces. In recent years, the United States has complained about the 'automatic majority' in the United Nations, consistently uses its veto to block decisions and actions, and walks out or threatens to walk out of UN agencies such as UNCTAD, ILO and UNESCO. There are even threats of total pullout from the UN, which is regarded as 'an enemy'.

[68] Linking aid and voting in the United Nations and elsewhere, Henry Kissinger stated: "The hostility of some of the Third World spokesmen and bloc voting have made constructive discussion in the UN forums between the industrial and developing world almost impossible. I have instructed each US Embassy that the factors by which we will measure the value which that government attaches to its relations with us will be its statements and its votes on that fairly limited number of issues which we indicate are of importance to us in international forums".

[69] Quoted in Peter H. Odegard and E. Allen Helms, *American Politics* Harper and Brothers, New York, p. 14.

[70] Ibid., p. 40.

[71] *Whence The Threat To Peace*, Moscow, 1984, p. 81.

[72] Quoted in A. Lebedv, S. Gribanov, op. cit., p. 23.

[73] Ibid

[74] Ibid

Cheddi Jagan inspects the troops as Commander-in-Chief of the Guyana Defence Force, July 1996

Cheddi Jagan at Hope Estate, East Coast Demerara, listening to people's problems, July 1994

Cheddi Jagan meets with the President of Botswana, Dr Quett Masire, during his State Visit to Guyana, 1994

Former United States President, Jimmy Carter meets members of Cheddi Jagan's Cabinet in Georgetown, April 1996

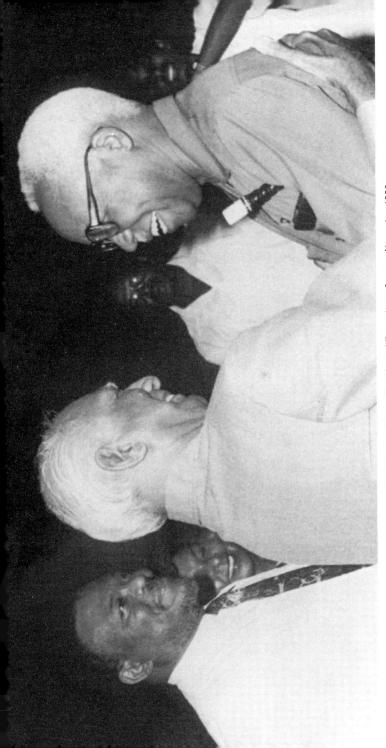

Cheddi Jagan and Prime Minister Sam Hinds welcome Julius Nyerere, former President of Tanzania, to Guyana, November 1996

Cheddi and Janet Jagan meet the UN Secretary General, Boutros Boutros-Ghali, 1st October 1993

Cheddi Jagan and the Director of UNICEF meet at United Nations Headquarters, October 1995

Cheddi Jagan addresses the UN World Food Summit in Rome, 13th-17th November 1996

Cheddi Jagan, Guyana's High Commissioner in London, Lall Singh, and Minister Jagdeo at a meeting in Brussels with the President of the European Community, Jaques Delors

An audience with the Pope at the Vatican, November 1996

Cheddi Jagan gives the keynote address at the 27th Annual Conference of the Association of Caribbean Historians at the University of Guyana, April 1995

Cheddi Jagan delivering the feature address at the Second Seminar on the Regional Development/Integration Fund, Georgetown, October 1996. Ministers Rohee and Sree Chand are on the panel

Cheddi Jagan addresses the 18th Annual Conference of the National Council for Black Studies which held its 2nd International Conference in Georgetown from the 1st - 4th June, 1994

Cheddi Jagan and the President of the TUC, October 1995

Cheddi Jagan presenting copies of his document, 'New Human Global Order' to the vice-chancellor of the University of Guyana, 5th February, 1995

Chapter Five

Anatomy of Electoral Fraud in Guyana

Fraud is a mild word to describe the motions which Guyana went through on December 16 ... these are only a part of the irregularities imposed on this country in what is wrongly called an election ... down the corridors of the centuries, this day will be remembered with shame."

That was how a former minister of the PNC/UF coalition government (1964-68), Randolph Cheeks, described the fraudulent 1968 general election. The fraud in the 1985 national and regional elections was even more blatant and disgraceful: the ruling People's National Congress (PNC), with the slogan "we can, we must, we will," took 79% of the votes cast.

Like Hitler's National Socialist Party which started out its murderous career as a minority party, the PNC had polled 41% of the votes in the 1964 elections. Since then, through massive fraud, at what are now called selections, the ruling party has taken a greater percentage of votes at each successive election - 56% in 1968; 70% in 1973; 78% in 1980.

With a severe economic and social crisis, declining living standards, deteriorating social services, shortage of basic essentials of life like flour, soap, edible oil, salt, etc., and exorbitant blackmarket prices, the ruling party could not have got in 1985 even the 21% of the votes it gave the opposition parties. Its real support was around half the amount allocated to the opposition.

The "overwhelmingly victory" of 42 out of 53 seats and 228,718 votes out of a total of 291,175 votes cast at the election, deemed by President Hoyte as "free, fair and above board," was a statistical absurdity. By no stretch of the imagination could the PNC in the twenty-one year period (1964-85) increase its support from 41% of the votes cast and twenty-two out of fifty-three seats in the National Assembly in 1964 to 79% and forty-two seats respectively in 1985.

CLASS AND RACE

The absurdity becomes clear when voter turnout and class and racial factors are taken into account.

The low turnout of voters in the capital, Georgetown, one of its former strongholds, is an indication of PNC weakness. Over the years, there has been a steady and precipitous decline - 90-95% in 1964; 60-65% in 1973; 12-15% in 1978.

In the 1978 referendum, there was a united boycott by all opposition parties and other civic groups. A monitoring of polling stations showed a voter turnout of only about 15%. Since then, the quality of life has deteriorated further. This deterioration was reflected in the growth within the TUC of the progressive bloc of four unions in 1977, six unions in 1983 and seven unions in 1984, the loss of PNC control of the Trades Union Congress (TUC) in 1984, and the TUC non-endorsement of the PNC in 1985, the first time in twenty-one years.

Class has now become the dominant factor in Guyanese politics. This was not so in 1964 when the PNC first came to power. Then, with the fomenting and financing of racial incitement, strife, strikes, arson and mayhem by the Central Intelligence Agency (CIA), racial violence and polarization had become complete. Race became the dominant factor in the 1964 elections, with the blacks supporting more or less the PNC, the Indians the People's Progressive Party (PPP) and the Amerindians the United Force (UF).

That class has become dominant was evidenced at the TUC Annual Conference in late 1984. Of the two-hundred and twelve delegates, about two-thirds of whom were black, eighty eight were accredited to the seven-union movement and one-hundred and twenty four to the seventeen unions controlled by the PNC. Despite this, the seven-union movement won the key positions for officers of the Executive Council, including the presidency.

To justify its "overwhelming victory" at the 1985 general and regional elections, President Desmond Hoyte claimed that the PNC had crossed the racial barrier.

This is ridiculous. It is not a new claim. His predecessor L F S Burnham had stated that in 1973 - the "Year of the Breakthrough" - the PNC had breached PPP strongholds in the Corentyne, Berbice, a predominantly Indian area. The falsity of that claim was demonstrated a few years later when, during the frame-up, on a charge of murder, of PPP activist Arnold Rampersaud, the government prosecution requested and obtained a transfer of the trial from Berbice to Georgetown on the ground that the jury would be prejudiced!

The Indians, who make up about fifty-two per cent of the population, are mainly workers and peasants. As such, there is no basis for a shift of their support from the PPP to the PNC. Under the latter's bureaucratic, state, co-operative and parasitic capitalism, now in alliance with the big local agricultural and industrial bourgeoisie, the Indian workers and peasants, like others of these class categories, have suffered tremendously, and have carried on a relentless struggle.

The sugar workers, largely Indian, struggled for over two decades to secure recognition of their union, the Guyana Agricultural and General Workers Union (GAWU). This was secured after a thirteen-week strike in 1975, two years after the so-called Year of the Breakthrough. In a secret poll with a high turnout of workers, GAWU won an overwhelming victory with 98% of the votes cast.

In a one-hundred and thirty-five day strike in 1977, the government mobilized 5000 scabs and coerced the military, paramilitary, civil servants, teachers and a fanatical black-dominated cult, the House of Israel, to crush the sugar workers and de-recognize GAWU. But it failed, as a result of regional and international solidarity, and the militancy and sacrifice of the workers.

And after the December 1985 rigged elections, the sugar industry was shut down in a two-day protest strike.

The absurdity of the election results is clear when it is noted that sugar workers and the adult members of their families alone constitute a much larger number than the total votes 'given' to all the opposition parties!

The farming community, which is largely Indian and Amerindian, has also suffered. This had led to an exodus from the countryside.

One-third of the rice farmers, mainly Indian, who, in the early 1960's constituted 54,000 families, have quit the industry, and large numbers of them have emigrated. One-third of the land under rice cultivation has been abandoned. In January 1986, a former PPP regional chairman disclosed that out of 46,000 acres of rice land in Region 5, only 12,000 had been cultivated.

This is due to the fact that for many years, rice cultivation by the small farmer has become uneconomic. According to a study by the International Fund for Agricultural Development (UFAD), the parasitic Guyana Rice Board, the state marketing organization, gave to the farmers only 47 cents of every dollar it earned overseas.

Simultaneously, the farmers are faced with interminable problems - poor drainage and irrigation; shortage of, and high prices for, inputs such as fertilizers, insecticides, bags, twine, machinery (tractors and harvesters). Even for the purchase at high prices of simple essential items such as a grass knife and cutlass, a permit must first be obtained. On the black-market, the price for a file and cutlass is about G$80 and for a grass knife G$75.

Yet the world is asked to believe that the farmers voted for the ruling party!

The marked deterioration in the quality of life of the Guyanese working people of all ethnic groups, including the blacks particularly since 1977, has led to a drastic fall in membership of the PNC and its arms. Henry Jeffrey, principal of the Kuru Kuru

Co-operative College, in his co-authored book *Guyana: Politics, Economics and Society*, disclosed that PNC membership dropped from 50,000 in 1973 to only 8,300 in 1983: its women's organization had only eight-hundred and twenty-five members and its youth movement a mere 357.

This is a reflection of the collapse of its grass-roots party structures and the dependence on the state bureaucracy for the manning of its electoral machinery and the rigging of the elections.

So barefaced was the rigging that the PPP was given only one-hundred and twenty-three votes for Region 1, but its list of candidates and sponsors alone totalled one-hundred and thirty-six. Another opposition party claimed that two-hundred and twenty persons with ID cards sponsored its list of candidates for Region 10, but it got only 62 votes. And the high figure of 95% of votes cast for the vast Northwest Region 1 was another statistical impossibility.

METHODS OF RIGGING

Electoral fraud ever since 1968 has been carried out by a combination of ways - an ineffectual Elections Commission; complete PNC control of the electoral machinery; overseas, proxy and postal voting; army intervention; tampering with ballot boxes.

The Elections Commission has become a 'toothless poodle' of the PNC. Much of its powers have been eroded, and whatever little power it retains is not exercised in the interest of fairness and impartiality.

The Constitution of Guyana (British Guiana) and the Election Regulations of 1964 placed full responsibility for the conduct and supervision of all phases of elections in the Elections Commission. It had overriding powers over all officials concerned with the administrative conduct of the elections, and could issue any directions it considered necessary or expedient for the purpose of ensuring impartiality and fairness.

The 1968 Representation of the People Act disabled the

Commission and placed some of its powers and functions in the Minister of Home Affairs and Chief Election Officer. The latter is torn between two masters: the Elections Commission and the Minister of Home Affairs, and generally takes instructions from the Minister.

Electoral rigging in past elections began with the compilation of the voters' lists. In 1964, the registration of voters was a function of the Elections Commission. To ensure fairness, political parties were allowed to appoint scrutineers, who were paid a small allowance and worked alongside the enumerators. Under the PNC government, voter registration was placed fully under its control. This led to massive padding with names of dead, emigrated, underage and non-existent persons; and also deliberate exclusion of names of voters in opposition strongholds.

The voters' lists were as follows: 298,939 (1953); 212,518 (1957); 246,120 (1961); 247,604 (1964); 369,088 including 68,000 overseas (1968); 421,575 (1973); 512,500 preliminary and 430,375 final, including 46,921 overseas (1980); 371,000 preliminary and 399,280 final, including 3,256 overseas (1985).

So padded were the 1968 lists that the number of voters increased by 20.9% (local) and 49% (local and overseas) over the 1964 registered voters. In 1973, the increase was 24.5% over 1968. The padding was apparent when official statistics showed an average population increase of only 2.5% per year.

In 1980, there was severe criticism of the huge preliminary lists of voters. These were supposedly 'published' (posted up) on October 27, but the PPP, the main opposition party, did not receive them until November 7: three days before the closing date for filing objections and claims - an impossible feat. Finally, 111,500 names were officially deleted and 29,379 were added, with no opportunity for revision!

In 1985, The Minister of Home Affairs refused to agree to the appointment, as in 1964, of scrutineers to work alongside the enumerators in the preparation of the national register. He also refused to agree to put the birthdates of persons, especially aged eighteen to twenty-five, on the preliminary list of voters, which was intended to be a safeguard against the padding of the voters lists with underage persons.

The padding was concentrated this time not so much in the preliminary list but in the supplementary list, which amounted to approximately 44,000 names, and with no opportunity for checking and revision.

The supplementary lists had been promised by the Chief Election Officer to the People's Progressive Party (PPP) about a week before election day. But they were not furnished. Lists totalling 17,000 for nine regions were given to the PPP on December 8, one day before the election. But the supplementary voters' list for Region 4 (including Georgetown, the capital), totalling about 27,000 was not supplied.

In response to protests, the stock answer was: the lists only had to be displayed in such places as the Minister prescribed, and there was no obligation on anyone to send or give a copy to any political party.

Proxy voting (and postal voting from 1973) was used to facilitate the casting of ballots for dead, emigrated, underage and non-existent persons appearing on the padded voters' lists.

In 1961, with the PPP in office, there were only about 300 proxies cast - persons designated to vote for another registered voter. This number increased to 6,635 in 1964, no doubt in order to help in ousting the PPP from the government for the PNC and its subsequent coalition partner got 90% of the proxies.

Under the PNC government, the figure for proxy votes in the 1968 elections was 19,287, equivalent to about three seats, but it was believed that the figure was much higher: the list of proxies was never published.

This method of electoral fraud was facilitated by changes in the law in 1964. The categories of persons entitled to vote by proxy was widened to exempt from direct voting those persons for whom it was likely to be impractical or seriously inconvenient for reason of the general nature of their occupations, service or employment, or for some good cause to go in person to the polling place at which they were entitled to vote. Also, proxy votes could now be cast for three other persons.

Because of the widespread criticism over the abuse of proxy and postal voting, and no doubt also for cosmetic reasons, shortly before the 1985 elections, postal voting was abolished and proxy voting restricted.

Overseas voting was first introduced in 1968. With a total of 68,000 mainly fictitious, overseas voters, the PNC "increased" its votes from 41% in 1964 to 56% in 1968, thus enabling it to expel its coalition partner, the United Force (UF), and to establish alone an administrative dictatorship.

A reputable London firm, the Opinion Research Centre, estimated in a survey that at least 72% of the entries on the UK electoral register were incorrect. In the prize-winning Granada TV film, "The Making of a Prime Minister," the Centre's director Humphrey Taylor disclosed that "the compilation of the register was a totally dishonest and corrupt operation... unprecedented for a Commonwealth country ... a pretty awful and disgraceful episode."

So disgraceful was the whole episode that the film showed two houses at a place in Manchester as the address of two fictitious voters Lily and Olga Barton; Gladys Foster was meant to live in a house in London which had been "demolished for the railway in 1874"; a law student Joe Hughes admitting that he had registered only forty-one persons in Wolverhampton, a London suburb, and doubting that over two-hundred could be on the voters' list.

The transcript of the film went on to say that "the newly-elected Prime Minister of Guyana, Forbes Burnham, arrives in London today (January 6, 1969) for the Prime Minister's Conference. He should not be attending."

For the 1973 overseas electoral lists, Granada Television film, "Mr Burnham Has Done It Again," showed Jamaicans, including children, were registered as voters. Two children's occupations were listed as clerk and fitter.

These exposés of the overseas fraudulent voters' lists caused great embarrassment. Consequently, the numbers of overseas voters were reduced from 68,000 in 1968 to 46,921 in 1980 and to 3,256 in 1985.

In restricting overseas and proxy voting and abolishing postal voting, President Desmond Hoyte said that he had met the main concerns of the opposition parties. This was not true.

The main concern of the opposition parties was the tampering with ballot boxes, which has been the decisive factor in the ruling party's "victories."

At the 1968 elections, for the Pomeroon District, Essequibo, four parcels of ballot papers bound with rubber bands and marked PNC, were found in a ballot box. When the Counting Agent for the United Force, Mr K D Doobay, a Barrister-at-Law, strenuously objected to the counting of this box, the Presiding Officer ordered that the ballot papers be replaced in the box and that it be handed over to the police at the police station for custody, until he received instructions from the Chief Election Officer in Georgetown. This was done and the next day the Presiding Officer sent messages to the counting agents that he had been instructed to proceed with the count. However, on this occasion when the box was opened it was found that the parcels of ballot papers with rubber bands were no longer marked for the PNC but for the UF, but since all the ballot papers were also found to be without the official stamp, they were deemed spoilt votes.

At the June 1970 local government elections, in District 23 of La Penitence-Lodge, 416 votes were cast, but the box had 573. In Division 128, 437 voted, but only 407 ballots were in the box. In District 17 of Division 2, 410 votes were cast but the box contained only 310. At Queen's College, because a previous decision was reversed, representatives of the People's Progressive Party (PPP) and the United Force could not observe the ballot counting, mainly by supporters of the ruling People's National Congress (PNC).

In 1973, when the ballot boxes emerged at the counting places, there were many indications of tampering: keys were misplaced and did not fit the boxes to which they had been attached when the boxes were sealed; the seals covering the slots of the ballot boxes were no longer present; the numbers of ballot papers in the boxes did not tally with the records of the presiding officers.

For example, in Demerara Coast West, in Division 2, the votes cast were 531, but 491 were in the ballot box when it finally emerged, after long hours, at the counting place. Division 1 had recorded 506 votes as being polled but the box had 527 votes! In some districts, there were more votes in the ballot boxes than electors listed as voters for the particular area. In the Northwest District, when the boxes were being emptied for counting, twenty-one wads of ballot papers, some with rubber bands and some with paper clips were revealed.

The tampering with ballot boxes was noted by the Chief Election Officer. In his Report of the 1973 Election, he wrote in paragraph 56 about "... the presence of a bundle of half-folded ballot papers that were taken from a ballot box ... There were many such bundles in several boxes for this district."

The 1980 general elections were the same, the Chief Election Agent, the Counting Agent and the Elections Commissioner of the PPP were kept away at gun point by the military from the places where the ballot boxes were stored. Counting began several hours later.

These and other factors caused the international team of observers, headed by British peer Lord Avebury, to say that "on the basis of abundant and clear evidence ... the election was rigged massively and flagrantly."

In 1985, President Desmond Hoyte assumed the role of a shining "Sir Galahad." On November 4, 1985, announcing some long overdue reforms and long fought-for concessions, he proclaimed that he was cutting the ground from "under the PPP and Jagan so that they will not have any credible base for complaint about 'rigged' elections."

However, he refused to agree to the counting of ballots at the place of poll, claiming that it had never been done in Guyana. Actually, it had not been done in the 1950's and early 1960's because there had been no charge of tampering with ballot boxes. He dismissed it as "a red herring and an irrelevance" and "something that is logistically difficult and unacceptable."

Erroneously, he declared that such a procedure would lead to three different counts - count at place of poll, at regional level and national level - and thus cause an interminable delay in the determination of the election results.

The delay nevertheless occurred. It took three days before the final results were announced. In contrast, in Nicaragua where votes were counted at the place of poll, results were obtained three to four hours after the end of polling.

As a gesture to mounting criticism, the President and the Minister of Home Affairs declared that polling agents of opposition parties would be allowed to accompany ballot boxes.

But the opposition was not taken in by this manoeuvre. It was apparent that the PNC could not win the elections without tampering with the ballot boxes. And if it was not prepared to have a preliminary count at the place of poll, it was not likely to implement the accompaniment of ballot boxes.

A previous commitment on this score had not been fulfilled. In 1973, the three opposition parties had approached the then Minister of Home Affairs for their agents to be in the same vehicles conveying the ballot boxes from the polling places to the counting place. It would be impracticable, he said. Finally, at the level of the Elections Commission, it was agreed that the three opposition parties would appoint one person to be in the vehicle or craft conveying the ballot boxes.

But this decision was not carried out. When the agreed polling agent of the parties presented his credentials, he was told by the presiding officer that he had received no instructions. When told about this, the Chief Election Officer, who had assured the parties that such instructions had been issued, refused to make public the decision by press and radio.

Consequently, the People's Progressive Party (PPP) sought guarantees from both the government and the Elections Commission about military non-involvement, the proper sealing of the ballot boxes, and the precise method of the accompaniment of ballot boxes from the polling places to counting places.

But these guarantees were not forthcoming. And new

methods of fraud were opened up under the electoral strategy embracing: (1) no international observers; (2) total control of the electoral machinery; (3) ejection of polling agents and the stuffing of ballot boxes; (4) military seizure of, and tampering with, ballot boxes.

For the first time, the disciplined forces (police, military and parliamentary) were permitted to vote with four options - vote by proxy; vote on a special day (December 3) before election day (December 9); vote on election day at place where registered; vote on election day at place other than where registered.

This new system partially replaced postal voting, which was abolished. But it opened the way to multiple voting, especially with PNC in total control of the election machinery.

The voters' lists for the disciplined forces, who voted on December 3 was never supplied to opposition parties. Nor were the lists of proxies. It was therefore impossible to monitor whether members of the disciplined forces voted more than once.

The lists of polling places for the disciplined forces were given only at 3 30 pm on December 2, the day before polling. Consequently, it was impossible to assign polling agents, particularly for the hinterland areas. The People's Progressive Party (PPP), for instance, was able to appoint, within that short period, polling agents at only 10 out of the 25 polling places.

Another new feature was the forceful ejection of opposition parties' polling agents at polling places, particularly in the capital Georgetown, and the bauxite mining towns of Linden and Kwakwani. This became necessary as a result of:

> 1) low turnout at outdoor meetings during the election campaign and of voters on the morning of election day in areas of PNC strength fifteen to twenty years ago, as compared with high turnout in PPP strongholds;

> 2) the restriction of overseas and proxy voting and the abolition of postal voting in 1985;

3) the difficulty of tampering with ballot boxes in Georgetown because of the concentration of regional and international journalists; this forced the armed forces to adopt a low profile in the capital. On the other hand, the armed forces were very visible and intimidatory elsewhere in manhandling ballot boxes and voters alike.

Opposition polling agents were generally not allowed to perform their duties and to accompany the ballot boxes. A large number were physically ejected from the polling places by PNC thugs. One PPP agent, after being kicked out, was told: "If you come back, you will have your grave here."

The ejection of the polling agents more than compensated for the restricted overseas and proxy voting and the abolished postal voting. It facilitated the stuffing of ballot boxes for dead, emigrated, underage, and non-existent persons whose names appeared on the padded supplementary lists, and for those who refused to turn out to vote for the ruling party.

At the end of polling, ballot boxes were seized by the security forces. Some polling agents were physically assaulted when they attempted to accompany the ballot boxes. And the boxes were kept out of sight of opposition parties' agents and candidates for long periods before counting began. The first result for Region 2 was announced twenty-four hours after polling. The other results were declared two or three days later. The long delay was required to permit tampering with the ballot boxes.

President Desmond Hoyte said the elections were "above board and regular." But his "overwhelming victory" was condemned by the opposition political parties, civic organizations and foreign journalists.

The Bishops of the Catholic and Anglican churches, along with other representatives of trade unions, the Bar Association and the Human Rights Association, expressed their "profound disappointment" over the way the elections were held, and recorded that "... the familiar and sordid catalogue of widespread disenfranchisement, multiple voting, ejection of polling agents, threats, intimidation, violence and collusion by police and army personnel characterised the poll..."

British journalist Anthony Jenkins, who thought he was "in danger of being lynched" when he and I had been mobbed by PNC gun-toting thugs at Haslington, East Coast Demerara, said that the "election was characterized by blatant fraud and intimidation."

The Guyanese people now have the task of intensifying the struggle for the following demands:

> 1) the dismissal of the Chairman of the Elections Commission and the reconstitution of the Elections Commission with an agreed independent chairman;
>
> 2) the dismissal of the Chief Election Officer and the nomination of a Chief Election Officer responsible to the independent Commission;
>
> 3) the preparation of new voters' lists by an independent Elections Commission;
>
> 4) the repeal of all laws and regulations made since 1967/68 so as to restore the functions and powers of the Elections Commission as laid down in the Constitution of Guyana and in the Election Regulations of 1964; the inclusion of another provision specifically calling for the counting of votes at the place of poll immediately after polling ceases;
>
> 5) the holding immediately under the auspices of the newly constituted Elections Commission of local government elections, which were last held (and rigged) in 1970;
>
> 6) the holding of new national and regional elections.

The prospects for the future are bright. The 1985 elections, though rigged as before, have seen a definite shift in the correlation of forces.

The ruling PNC is more isolated from the mass of the working people than ever before, and this will deepen. Its support is becoming more and more restricted to the party die-hards and faithfuls to whom it can dispense patronage, and to the big businessmen, who are becoming multimillionaires under state capitalism and contraband trading. Prior to 1977, the PNC maintained power not only through fraud, force and fear but also by political patronage and racial and political discrimination. However, since 1978, particularly with the IMF agreement and the parlous state of the economy, it began to put pressures on its former supporters. This brought about the objective conditions for mass struggles and the creation of working-class and racial unity.

The people's forces struggling for democracy and bread are growing. The tempo of consolidation is quickening, particularly at the level of political parties, the trade unions, the farmers' organizations and the Church. These forces are now banding themselves into the Patriotic Coalition for Democracy (PCD).

The PCD is committed to struggle for the restoration of the fundamental rights in the Guyana Constitution and the United Nations Covenant on Civil and Political Rights.

Developments regionally and internationally also favour the Guyanese people's struggle.

There has been universal condemnation in the Caribbean of the electoral fraud. In Latin America, the process of democratization is gaining ground, the most recent manifestation being the downfall of 'Baby Doc' Duvalier. And the Gorbachev/Reagan talks open new prospects for disarmament, detente, peaceful coexistence and world peace.

February 1986 (*Toronto South Asian Review*)

Appendix

LETTER FROM PREMIER CHEDDI JAGAN TO PRESIDENT JOHN F KENNEDY[1]
GEORGETOWN, APRIL 16, 1963

Dear Mr President,

It will be recalled that as a result of my talks with you and US Government officials in October 1961, your Government in response to my request for aid, undertook to take the following steps:

1. (i) To provide as early as possible in consultation with the British Guiana Government, and unilaterally or in co-operation with Hemisphere organizations, economists and other experts to assist the Government of British Guiana to bring the most modern economic experience to bear upon the reappraisal of its development programme.

(ii) To provide technical assistance for feasibility, engineering and other studies concerning specific development projects.

(iii) To determine as soon as possible after the steps mentioned in paragraphs one and two, and on the submission of suitable projects within the context of the British Guiana Development Plan, what assistance the US can give in financing such projects, taking into account other US commitments, available financial resources, and the criteria established by applicable legislation.

(iv) To expand its existing technical assistance.

2. In the period since my visit, US technical assistance has been expanded, and feasibility and engineering studies for certain specific development projects are in train. On the other hand progress with the reappraisal of the development programme has been far less satisfactory. Following on the cancellation of its proposed visit early in February, the Economic Planning team led by Mr Harry G Hoffman eventually visited British Guiana in May of last year. It is now very nearly a year since the visit of that mission but I have so far been unable to obtain any certain information regarding the progress of its report. (It is understood however that when the AID Desk Officer visited British

Guiana two months ago he stated in a newspaper interview that the Mission's report had then been sent to the printer.) I am naturally anxious about the fate of the Hoffman report as it appears that US assistance in the financing of development project is conditional on the completion of it.

3. My request for aid in October 1961 was only the latest request of the many made over the years for US assistance with development projects. Early in 1958, an application was made to the Development Loan Fund (DLF) for aid for financing road and drainage and irrigation projects. I visited Washington in the summer of 1958 and 1959 and held talks with officials of the World Bank and US Government Agencies. At a meeting with State Department officials in 1959 in Washington, I was told that a sum of about $6 to $8 million (US) would be made available to my Government toward the cost of the construction of an interior road from Parika to Lethem. Such aid did not in fact materialize. A request was also made to the Commodities Division Office of International Resources in the State Department to see if this country's imports of flour and stock-feed from the USA ($3.5 million US per annum) might be given under United States Public Law 480 and the proceeds of the sale used for development projects. This request was turned down as it was explained that any assistance under the law must be over and above the existing volume of imports. The Export-Import Bank was then asked to assist with the financing of equipment for a flour mill and a feed mill but the response was not encouraging.

4. At one stage a US AID official in British Guiana indicated that economic assistance might be forthcoming for a Land Reclamation Project (the Tapacuma Drainage and Irrigation Scheme). But later, when the Project Report was ready my Government was informed that assistance was not likely to be available because of possible Congressional objections to a scheme which would be solely devoted to the cultivation of rice, a commodity of which the US had a large surplus.

5. An application to the Export-Import Bank in June 1961 for rice milling equipment - cleaning, drying and storage - amounting to about $2 million BWI has not yet been considered.

6. It will thus be seen, that leaving technical assistance aside, valuable though such assistance is, my efforts to obtain US assistance have so far yielded little material result. It was against a background of growing unemployment and lack of adequate overseas assistance that I resolved on my return to British Guiana from the USA in November, 1961, to embark on a programme of fiscal reform designed to mobilise local resources for development. I was encouraged in this

step by the fact that the criteria for AID assistance appeared to stress self-help efforts by the less developed countries themselves. I had noted that it had been stated in the Summary Presentation of an Act for International Development, 1961 (page 14) that the major areas of self-help include "The effective mobilizing of resources. This includes not only development programming, but also establishing tax policies designed to raise equitable resources for investment; fiscal and monetary policies designed to prevent serious inflation, and regulatory policies aimed to attract the financial managerial resources of foreign investment and to prevent excessive luxury consumption by a few."

7. Unfortunately this self-help or austerity budget was used as an excuse for disturbances inspired by opponents of the Government. These disturbances have since been thoroughly investigated by a Commonwealth Commission of Inquiry and it is worth recording the views of that Commission on the Budget: "It will be seen" stated the Commission on page 15 of its report "that there was nothing deeply vicious or destructive of economic security in the budget. It had been drawn up on the advice of an experienced economist, who could not be said to have any Communist prepossessions. The budget won immediate approval from many persons. *The New York Times* said in an editorial that the budget was courageous and economically sound. *The London Times* in a leading article observed 'The immediate problem for the Prime Minister, Dr Jagan, is how to win some acceptance for his economic proposals which are courageous and certainly not far from what Guiana must have.' Sir Jock Campbell, Chairman of Booker Bros., the largest industrial and agricultural concern in British Guiana, said 'It clearly was in intention a serious attempt by the Government to get to grips with the formidable economic problems of the country by a hard programme of self-help. It was radical - what have the people of British Guiana got to be conservative about - but not confiscatory.' Senator Anthony Tasker, Chairman of Bookers Group Committee in British Guiana, gave his own opinion about the budget by saying 'We assessed it as a realistic attempt to grapple with the economic problems of British Guiana.'"

8. I venture to suggest that an objective consideration of these Budget proposals and the overall programme of my Government leads to the conclusion that they meet, to a high degree, the criteria which have been laid down by your Government for disbursements under the Alliance for Progress:

(a) *Long range plans based on the application of programming techniques must be drawn up for both private and public sectors:*

My country as compared with many under-developed territories has had a comparatively long history in the planning of economic development. A development programme prepared as long ago as 1948 by the then Economic Adviser to Government the UK economist Col. O A Spencer, introduced ideas which later influenced planning within the Caribbean region and exercised a considerable influence in other British colonial territories. In 1952-1953 a Mission from the World Bank considered afresh and reported on the problems of the economic development of the territory. Then in 1959 a Cambridge University Economics Don, Mr Kenneth Berrill, at the request of my Government, advised on the preparation of the Development Programme which is now in progress. My Government has also had from time to time the benefit of the advice of many distinguished economic experts who have visited for short periods. It will thus be seen that the Hoffman Mission is only the most recent study of our economic problems.

(b) *The fiscal system should be reformed both in order to increase the level of tax revenue in relation to national income and to make the tax structure more progressive. At the same time the machinery for the collection and assessment should be completely overhauled:*

This was what the budget of 1962 mainly sought to do. It is also to be noted that this budget reflects the major conclusions reached at the Conference on Fiscal Policy held in Santiago, Chile last December and which was attended by fiscal experts from all over the Americas. In a release made in Washington by the Pan American Union Secretariat of the Organization of American States it was stated among other things that it had been agreed that the reform of Latin American tax system should include progressive personal income tax which included the taxation of capital gains both on mobile and immobile property, complemented by a net wealth tax where feasible and the strengthening of a system of inheritance and gift taxation. Those recommendations also envisaged the establishment of an objective and co-ordinated system of tax administration - all features of my 1962 Budget. This budget also proposed a number of measures including Pay-As-You-Earn which were calculated to improved the efficiency of tax collection and to prevent tax evasion. Although certain of the budget proposals were subsequently withdrawn the present position is that all the fiscal requirements mentioned have been met.

(c) *Measures should be instituted to increase domestic savings and these should be applied to productive investment*:

The budget already referred to introduced a National Development Savings Levy: Under this scheme, persons earning more than $300 a month (a better than middle class salary) are asked to contribute 5% of that part of their incomes above $300 to a National Savings Scheme. The scheme also applies to companies which contribute 10% of their income before tax. The monies which accrue in this way are safeguarded by being directly chargeable on the revenues and assets of the country, and are being put into development fund and drawn upon for the financing of concrete and high earning schemes calculated to have an immediate impact on development, especially in the urban areas.

(d) *Certain basic social reforms must be implemented such as the breaking up of large latifundia - the old plantation type economy - for the purpose of distributing unused or under-utilized land to peasants who will be required to put the land to good use:*

Since 1957, my Government has succeeded in persuading the foreign owned sugar companies to release some of their non-utilized lands leased from the Crown. Attempts are still being made to secure additional lands for use by individual farmers. The distribution of unused land to individual farmers is one of the objectives of my Government and has been pursued constantly. Nevertheless, the problem in this country is not one of maldistribution but of lack of financial resources to bring undeveloped land into cultivation.

(e) *The people Development programmes should lay as much stress on improving the quality of, for example by expenditure on education and training, as on increasing the stock of physical capital:*

My Government is now embarked on an educational programme which aims at promoting a national system of education which will provide all Guianese with the opportunity of developing their educational and personal potential and of sharing in all the educational facilities available regardless of race religion or economic circumstances. To this end the educational system is being reorganised - so as to provide for secondary and university education, after the pattern of your own country, for all who can benefit from it. My Government has also gone a long way towards providing health facilities throughout the country and a start has been made in certain areas on the provision of free medical services for the people.

(f) *Democratic regimes in Latin America should be encouraged:*

I have achieved power in the political life of my country by virtue of three successive General Elections which my Party won. I have often stated and now wish to re-affirm my adherence to parliamentary democracy by which I recognize the rights of opposition parties, freedom of speech, freedom of worship, regular and honest elections, an impartial judiciary and an independent public service. The draft constitution which my government proposed for an independent Guyana specifically provided for the protection of the rights of citizens by the Courts of Law along the lines enshrined in the US Constitution and moreover provided for the impartial conduct of elections and the review of boundaries of constituencies by an Electoral Commission. On this point may I venture to remind you of remarks ascribed to you in a USIS release of the 7th December, 1961. In the course of your interview with the Editor of *Izvestia* you are reported to have said "... the United States supports the idea that every people should have the right to make a free choice of the kind of Government they want... Mr Jagan ... who was recently elected Prime Minister in British Guiana is a Marxist, but the United States doesn't object because that choice was made by honest election, which he won."

(g) *Aid should be guaranteed over the period of the plan:*

I have long supported this idea as it is only on this basis that the Government of any under-developed country can plan development on sound lines.

9. Trade Policy

As the trade policy of my Government and its attitude to private enterprise has been widely and deliberately misrepresented in the USA I should like to deal briefly with these subjects. I am aware that the thinking which inspired your Act for International Development recognized the trade problems of the less developed countries. Thus on page 25 of the Summary Presentation already referred to, it is stated inter alia:

"Export capacities of most of the less developed countries are limited. In many cases, especially in Latin America and Africa, exports are heavily dependent on one or two primary products of either agricultural or mineral origin. For most of these products, world markets are expanding only slowly. The prices of these products are subject to volatile fluctuations which greatly affect the exchange available to producing countries. In some instances there appears to be a long-range trend for prices of primary commodities to fall in comparison with the prices of the industrial goods for which they must be exchanged. Moreover, the advance of science and technology presents for some commodities the prospect of displacement by synthetics (as had happened in some measure for rubber) or competition from substitutes."

It is these considerations which compel nations such as my own as a matter of economic necessity to seek markets or capital equipment wherever they may be obtained most advantageously. Such trading arrangements do not mean however that my Government has become part of any international conspiracy.

10. Attitude to Private Enterprise

My Government is committed to a mixed economy in which private and public enterprise would exist side by side as is the case with India. For reasons inherent in the nature of this county, my Government must enter as quickly as possible into the industrial sector of development, either alone or in joint ventures with private enterprise. It is however the policy of my Government to give protection where necessary to new undertakings both public and private, in order to make them viable and competitive.

11. The expropriation of private property is not in my Government's programme. The provisions for safeguarding the Fundamental Rights in our present Constitution and in the Constitution for an independent Guyana will provide adequate protection for private property.

12. On nationalization, no Government can tie its hands but it is not our intention to nationalize the bauxite and sugar industries. I am also prepared to guarantee that if any private enterprise should be nationalized there will be adequate and fair compensation to be decided by the Supreme Court of Law in cases of dispute as laid down in the Constitution.

13. A United Kingdom, Trade and Industrial Mission led by the English Industrialist Lord Rootes, which visited British Guiana in 1962 concluded that:

"On the political front, there is no exceptional risk to be faced by industry in British Guiana beyond that of nationalization inherent in any socialist country. It must be said also that sound reasons can be found in the condition of the country for Dr Jagan's concept of a mixed economy, with the Government providing some of the initiative in development."

14. Again as recently as March this year, Sir Jock Campbell, Chairman of Bookers Bros. McConnell and Company Limited, a group of companies which represent one of the large investments of private capital in this country, while on a visit stated that he saw no danger of a Communist dictatorship being established in British Guiana. He was confident that the Premier, Dr Jagan had no intention of setting up such a dictatorship and further, that the conditions were not present in British Guiana to make a communist dictatorship viable. "I do not

believe," Sir Jock Campbell said, "that there is a corrupt Government now in British Guiana against which the people will rebel and I do not think that the people can feel that they will be better off if there was a Communist Government." He added, however, that he did not think the people of British Guiana would vote for a Government whose stated policy was to pander to private enterprise.

15. In my country, we are now embarked on the creation of a just society based on the ideas and forms most suitable to the needs of this country and which would enable its citizens to develop themselves to the full in a free country. We have nothing to hide. Because of hostile, uninformed and unsympathetic speeches and comments made in the US Congress and press, I have already invited through your Consul General in Georgetown, members of Congress and of the press to visit from time to time. Such visits would be welcome. I cannot but think that the American people who first began that revolution in social and political thought which still moves our world will find sympathy with the ideas and aspirations of my people and Government.

16. As I am sure you are aware, a Government such as mine has inherited the problems of poverty and under-development which are characteristic of colonial territories. To these problems have been added the problem of a high post-war population growth. In the face of growing unemployment and all that it means in discontent and the waste of human resources, the political Opposition and other local leaders hostile to the Government have openly charged that US assistance will not be forthcoming once my Government remains in office. The long delay in the completion of the Hoffman Report has tended to lend substance to this charge. In addition, the Trade Union Congress which on the whole aligns itself with the political Opposition has recently announced that it has been able to arrange substantial assistance for a housing scheme through the American Institute for Free Labour Development, a body which, one senior local Trade Union Official stated in a broadcast, derives the major part of its funds from the Agency for International Development. Earlier a generous Scholarship Scheme announced by the US Consul General had apparently been designed to bypass my Government which had not been notified or taken into consultation.

17. These are only the most recent of the series of events which have created the impression that your Government is unwilling to assist the presently elected Government of this country and has served to embolden the Opposition to embark on irresponsible courses which are aimed at the forcible overthrow of my Government and which are

likely to undermine the future of democratic government and the maintenance of peace in this country.

18. Thus, US citizens, Dr Schwartz and Dr Sluis openly interfered in the domestic affairs of the country during the 1961 election campaign when they supported the Defenders of Freedom and the United Force. They later admitted spending the sum of about $76,000 BWI during this campaign. (It is to be noted that Section 53 of Cap. 57 - the Representation of the People Ordinance 1957 - limits the expenses which may be incurred by a candidate to $1,500 and there were only 35 seats.) Dr Sluis visited British Guiana six times between 21st February, 1961 and 26th April, 1962, including a two-month visit just prior to and during the 1961 Elections.

19. You will recall that I complained to you about the activities of US Government Information Services during the 1961 election campaign when film shows were held at street corners. The USIS had never before arranged for such shows in the public. These film shows highlighted anti-Castro and anti-communist propaganda. It happened that this line of propaganda coincided with the smear campaign then being conducted against the Government by the Opposition.

20. While no economic assistance was given to the Government, the impression was and is still being created in the country by Mr Peter D'Aguiar and the United Force that they will be able to secure substantial financial assistance from the US Government. During the election campaign the United Force cited a figure of one billion dollars, half a billion dollars as loans to the Government for "infra structure" development and half a billion for industrial development by private US investors. So far as I am aware, these statements met with no denial from your Consulate General, or any other US official.

21. Press reports had stated that Dr Claude Denbo, President of the League of Coloured Peoples and close associate of the People's National Congress had contacted, during a visit to the USA immediately prior to the 1961 August elections, a group of prominent Guianese professional men now resident in New York, some of whom had interviews with State Department officials at which, it was reported offers of assistance were made to help the Opposition to "liberate" British Guiana from my Government.

22. Since the elections it appears to be the policy of the United States State Department to refuse visas to members and known supporters of the governing party, People's Progressive Party, who wish to visit the United States. This has been the case even with well-known and eminently respectable members of the business community.

23. I cite these observations because I share your deep concern not only about the problems of world poverty but also of the growing tendency of the usurpation by reactionary elements of the democratic rights and liberties of free peoples. I am sure you would not want it said that in British Guiana, the objectives of your administration were not being realized and fulfilled.

24. In the light of the points made above I shall be grateful if urgent consideration may once again be given to the question of what assistance may be made available for the financing of development projects.

25. I have noted that you have been able in spite of the heavy burden of your office to visit a number of Latin American countries, so as to meet their people and to find out at first hand about their problems. I am aware that my own small country must rate low on the scale of priorities, but my Government nevertheless wishes to invite you to visit this country as soon as may be convenient to you. In the meanwhile my Government wishes to invite your personal aide, Mr Arthur Schlesinger Jr. who I understand has been entrusted with the study of the problems of this country to visit us as soon as possible.

Yours sincerely,

Cheddi Jagan

[1] Source: Kennedy Library, National Security Files, Countries Series, British Guiana III Secret. Transmitted to McGeorge Bundy by W.H. Brubeck on May 18 under cover of a note that indicates an advance copy of the letter was sent to the White House on May 1 and that the Department of State would submit a recommendation concerning a reply as soon as possible.

Index of Proper Names

Adams, T 87
Alfonsin, R 138
Allende, S 67, 68, 99
Arbenz, J 85, 136
Armas, Colonel 41

Ball, G 25
Barre, S 53
Barton, L & O 154
Batista, F 66
Beard, C 136
Berrill, K 166
Bevan, A 13
Bird, V 86
Bishop, M 117
Bolivar, S 136
Borm, W 72
Brandt, W 73
Brezezinski, Z 50, 57, 110, 112
Brezhnev, L 131, 132, 134
Bright, J 136
Brubeck, W 172
Bundy, M 172
Burnham, L F S 15, 17, 18, 19, 25, 71, 149, 154

Cabot, J 123
Cabral, A 74
Camara, D 27

Campbell, J 165, 169
Carter, J 18, 48, 50, 53, 57, 99, 109, 110, 112-114, 132, 134
Carter, R 49
Castro, F 29, 52, 53, 74
Chamberlain, M 136
Charles, E 73
Cheeks, R 147
Chernanko, K 137
Churchill, W 17, 41, 54, 100
Cobden, R 136
Coolidge, C 103

D'Aiguar, P 15, 171
D'Escoto, M 122
Dare, J 18
De Gaulle, C 128
Denbo, C 171
Diderot, D 136
Doobay, K 155
Dulles, J F 38, 48, 50, 59, 107, 109, 117, 128

Echeverria, L 90
Eisenhower, D 107, 128
Enders, T 122

Feinburg, R 113
Fernandes, J 18, 21

Ford, G 49, 99
Foster, G 154

Gairy, E 84
Gallegos, R 40
Gandhi, I 74, 137
Gladstone, W 136
Gomes, L 40
Grey, R 15

Habib, P 58
Haig, A 120
Hennessy, A 4
Hoffman, H 163
Hoyte, D 147, 155, 156, 159
Hughes, J 154

Jagan, J 13, 17
Jefferson, T 136
Jeffrey, H 150
Jenkins, A 160
Jiminez, M 40
Johnson, L B 32, 49, 108, 109, 127

Kendall, R 18
Kennedy, J F 19, 48, 49, 107, 109, 119, 127
Kirkpatrick, J 120
Kissinger, H 57, 112

Lafayette, M 102
Lehman, J 118
Lenin, N 93
Lucian 24
Luckhoo, L 18

Lumumba, P 44
Luyt, R 15
Lyons, J 125

MacArthur, D 128
MacCabe, H 14
Macmillan, H 14, 19
Madrid, Miguel de la 138
Malliard, W 13
Manley, M 49, 50
McCarthy, E 106, 128, 131
Melman, B 126
Minh, Ho Chi 74
Mossadegh, M 75
Munroe, J 35, 60, 102

Nasser, G 74
Nehru, J 41, 42
Neto, A 74
Nixon, R 48, 49, 63, 108, 128, 131, 138
Nkrumah, K 74
Nyerere, J 138

O'Keefe, J 15

Palme, O 138
Papandreou, A 138
Pearson, D 19
Perez de Cuellar, X 133
Pipes, R 117

Rao, R 51
Reagan, R 50, 58, 62, 73, 81, 82, 86, 90, 99, 110, 115, 117, 121, 124, 132, 138